MW00477025

SIN AND
SALVATION

By the same author

A South India Diary
The Household of God

SIN AND SALVATION

★

LESSLIE NEWBIGIN
Bishop in Madura and Ramnad

Wipf & Stock
PUBLISHERS
Eugene, Oregon

Wipf and Stock Publishers
199 W 8th Ave, Suite 3
Eugene, OR 97401

Sin and Salvation
By Newbigin, Lesslie
Copyright©1956 by Newbigin, Lesslie
ISBN 13: 978-1-60608-582-0
Publication date 4/7/2009
Previously published by SCM, 1956

CONTENTS

Preface   7

I   WHAT DO WE MEAN BY SALVATION?   11

   (a) Man is in a state of contradiction against the
      natural world   11
   (b) Man is in a state of contradiction against his
      fellow-man   12
   (c) Man is himself in a state of inner self-contradiction 13
   (d) Man is in a state of contradiction against God   13

II   WHAT IS SIN?   1. HOW DID IT ENTER THE

   WORLD?   16

   (a) God created man in His own image   16
   (b) God gave the world which He had created to man
      to enjoy, but He placed a limit   18
   (c) Man, wishing to be like God, transgresses that limit
      and falls into sin   19
   (d) As the result of his disobedience, man is driven
      from the presence of God and comes under a
      curse   21

III   WHAT IS SIN?   2. THE NATURE OF SIN   23

   (a) Sin is a corruption of the very centre of human
      nature   23
   (b) The root of sin is unbelief   25
   (c) Unbelief, anxiety, and the lie   26
   (d) Idolatry   27
   (e) Sensuality and lust   28
   (f) Envy, strife and murder   30

IV   THE SITUATION WHICH SIN HAS PRODUCED   32

   (a) The results of sin are real and terrible   32
   (b) Guilt and responsibility   34
   (c) Corporate guilt, original sin, and temptation   36
   (d) Man cannot save himself from sin   40

5

V THE PREPARATION FOR SALVATION 43

    (a) The story of salvation the story of actual events 43
    (b) The election of a people 43
    (c) The preparation for Christ 46
        1. The Prophet 47
        2. The Priest 49
        3. The King 52
    (d) The clue to the Old Testament 53

VI THE WORK OF THE SAVIOUR 56

    (a) Introduction 56
    (b) The teaching of Jesus about His death 62
        1. His death is necessary 62
        2. His death is the will of the Father 63
        3. His death arises from his identification of Him-
           self with sinners 64
        4. His death is God's judgment of the world 65
        5. His death is a ransom 66
        6. His death is a sacrifice 66
        7. His death is the means of life to the world 67
        8. His death is not to be an isolated event, but
           others are to follow it and share it 68
    (c) The death of Jesus a revelation of God's love 70
    (d) The death of Jesus as a judgment 73
    (e) The death of Jesus as ransom 80
    (f) The death of Jesus as sacrifice 83
    (g) The death of Jesus as victory 88
    (h) The resurrection and ascension of Jesus 90

VII HOW SALVATION BECOMES OURS 92

    (a) The Church 92
    (b) Word, sacrament, prayer, fellowship 94
    (c) The work of the Spirit 96
    (d) Faith 97
    (e) Regeneration 100
    (f) Justification 104
    (g) Growth in holiness 110

VIII THE CONSUMMATION OF SALVATION 115

    (a) The Christian hope 115
    (b) The coming again of Christ 117
    (c) Judgment 118
    (d) Resurrection 120
    (e) The kingdom of God 124

Index of Biblical References 126

PREFACE

THIS small book was originally published in Tamil for the use of church workers in the Tamil dioceses of the Church of South India. Those for whom it was intended are mostly village teachers of elementary grade, who—although without theological training—have to bear a heavy share of the responsibility for the pastoral care of several thousand village congregations in the Tamil country. To assist them in the discharge of this responsibility there is a carefully planned scheme of study and annual examination, for which purpose four new books are published each year dealing with different books of the Bible and different aspects of Christian faith and practice. The Editor of the Religious Book Club has been kind enough to suggest that this book might be of value to members of the Club and I have gladly agreed to its being published in English, but I hope that the reader will be kind enough to remember those for whom it was originally written.

I began writing it in Tamil but found that the work was proceeding too slowly and therefore completed it in English, and requested a friend to translate it. I have therefore tried to write the kind of English sentences that would go easily into Tamil, and have had all the time in mind the necessities of translation. I would beg the reader to be kind enough to remember this also.

Moreover, as regards substance I have tried to deal with the particular misunderstandings and perplexities which are common to Tamil Christians—which are by no means the same as those common in England. The words used in the Tamil Bible to translate 'sin' and 'salvation' are both unfortunate. The word *pavam*, which is used for 'sin', carries much less of the idea of personal guilt and responsibility and much more of the idea of misfortune than is proper for an equivalent of the biblical word 'sin'. And the word *ratchippu* means primarily providing support and sustenance. Dr J. H. Maclean of Conjeeveram, that great missionary of the Church of Scotland, used to say that the real meaning of the words used in the Tamil Bible at I Timothy 1.15 is 'Christ Jesus came into the world to provide free board and lodging for rascals'. The Hindu observer of our multitudinous philanthropic activities— and of our churches—is apt to think that he has understood that text. It is for this reason that I have tried to open up a fresh understanding of the meaning of the word ' salvation ' by tracing its connection with the Sanskrit root meaning 'wholeness'—a root which occurs in very many words commonly used in Tamil. One friendly critic has asked whether it is justifiable to define salvation in terms of 'making whole', and perhaps my treatment may be less than satisfactory at this point; but I think it was justifiable in the light of this common Tamil misunderstanding, and in the light of the Bible teaching as a whole, to adopt this approach to the subject in a book intended for simple people.

If one believes, as I do, that the phrase 'the finished work of Christ' stands for a precious and indispensable truth; if—in other words—one believes that something objective and final was done on Calvary for the whole relationship between the world and God, then the crucial point of difficulty is the answer to the question 'How does salvation become ours?' When I came to write that chapter I found that I had to make a decision about the order of the sections. In the tradition in which I was

brought up it would be normal to begin with a section on
'Faith' and work through to a (probably brief) concluding
section on the Church. After a good deal of reflection I
decided to reverse the order. Perhaps it does not matter
greatly whether one begins with the outward and visible
and moves to the inward and spiritual, or whether one
proceeds in the reverse direction. But there seem to me to
be two good reasons for the order I have adopted. Firstly,
it is the order which the reader of the New Testament
finds himself following: the Acts of the Apostles come
before the Epistles—the fact of the Church before the clue
to its inner life. Secondly, it is the order which the non-
Christian has to follow when he comes to Christ. What
he sees is a visible congregation in his village. It is that
congregation which holds out to him the offer of salvation. Only when he has come within its fellowship does
he (usually) come to any deep understanding of its inner
source.

I have to confess that the book was written under
severe pressure of time, and under the obligation to complete it by the date required for the Workers' Study
Scheme. Most of it was written away from home, and
therefore without books of reference. I have not attempted
to acknowledge obligation to the books which I have read
on this subject, except that—since the Palk Straits are
narrow—I have thought it proper to confess one piece of
burglary from the ample treasures of my friend Dr D. T.
Niles. I should also say that, shortly before starting to
write this, I had the privilege of going through the manu-
script of Dr Sigrid Estborn's book *The Christian Doctrine
of Salvation* for the Christian Students' Library. This book
stimulated my thinking a great deal, especially on the
points where I disagreed with Dr Estborn, and this has
certainly left its mark on the present work.

It remains only to say that I have not been able to see the typescript since it was sent home to the SCM Press. I have to leave it entirely in their hands, and I am grateful for all the care and devotion with which they always deal with such matters. I hope that this small book may help others to enter more fully into the mystery and joy of our common salvation.

LESSLIE NEWBIGIN
Bishop.

Madurai
March 1956

Publisher's note

Owing to the necessity of going to press with Religious Book Club books within a fixed time limit, we have not been able to incorporate the author's corrections in this book. Proofs were corrected by Bishop Newbigin but were lost in the mail from India to this country.

I

WHAT DO WE MEAN BY SALVATION?

WHEREVER and whenever we look at man, we find that he is full of self-contradiction. He is divided against himself, and he is divided against his environment. He is not at peace in himself, and he is not at peace with the world. If we try to examine this state of self-contradiction further, we shall find that there are four distinct ways in which man is in a state of contradiction.

(a) Man is in a state of contradiction against the natural world

Man is a part of the natural world. His body is made up of flesh, blood, bones and other constituents which are the same as those in many animals. Like them, he depends for his existence upon the correct kind of food, water, air, temperature etc., and if these are absent he dies.

But man is not at peace with the natural world. Of course, like other animals he is engaged in a struggle for existence which leads him to kill other animals for food, and to protect himself from other animals by force and cunning. This kind of conflict is found throughout the natural world, and man is also involved in it.

But there is more than this. Man has a different relation to the natural world from that which other animals have.

In the first place, man has tried to subdue the natural world to his will in a way that no animal has done. He has tamed animals and turned them to his use, cultivated plants, exploited the resources of the earth and the sea, discovered how to make and control fire, electric power, and atomic energy. But in spite of this, there is not peace between man and nature. For, in the second place, man's desires are such that nature cannot satisfy them. If an animal is given sufficient food, water, shelter, and opportunities for reproduction, it will be satisfied. But man is not satisfied with these things. He is tormented by desires which are unlimited, and therefore—not understanding the nature of his desires—he tries to get more of the same natural goods, and as a result becomes a glutton, a drunkard, or a sexual pervert. Because man is so made that only God can satisfy him, his desires are unlimited. When he tries to satisfy unlimited desires by means of natural goods, he ruins himself.

(b) Man is in a state of contradiction against his fellow-man

About this it is not necessary to write very much. From the time of Cain and Abel men have fought with one another, hated one another, murdered one another. Wherever we look we see strife: nation against nation, class against class, race against race, and—even in the same household—brother against brother and children against parents. Although all men know that this strife can bring only ruin and misery, although they know that without co-operation we must perish, although they know that love is the highest good and that without it life is not worth living, yet men fight one with another. Each one seeking his own good rather than the good of others, is brought up against others who are seeking their own good.

Each one sees the other as a threat to himself. So man is divided against man, and the human race, instead of being one united family, is constantly torn by fratricidal strife.

(c) Man is himself in a state of inner self-contradiction

Each man in himself is not a unity. His mind is a republic in which many forces are battling against one another. There are powerful instinctive forces which try to revolt against the sovereignty of his mind. His body is by no means always the obedient instrument of his will. And within his mind itself there are conflicting desires. Fears, ambitions, envies, hatreds arise in his mind which conflict with one another and with his own purposes, and threaten to ruin him. Above all, there is in every man a great division between what he knows he ought to do, and what he actually does. As St Paul says: 'The good which I would, I do not; but the evil which I would not, that I practise'.[1] In some degree or other this self-contradiction between what he is and what he knows he ought to be, runs through every man's soul. Man is himself a self-contradiction.

(d) Man is in a state of contradiction against God

This is the basic contradiction on which all else rests. Man is a creature in revolt against his creator, a creature who has cut himself off from the roots of his own being. That is why he is in a state of contradiction with the whole creation including himself. Man is made in God's image, for God, in order to do God's will; but he does not wish to do God's will. He thus tries to contradict his own essential nature. He is created in God's image, in order to live as God's child, in humble, trusting obedience. But he chooses to live otherwise, independent of God, relying on

[1] Rom. 7.19.

his own strength, his own wisdom and his own virtue. Even when he says 'I will walk in accordance with God's will', he wishes to do so in his own right and his own strength, not glorifying God but glorifying himself. He does not wish to seek only God's glory, but rather his own righteousness. This contradiction between man and God is the root of all the other contradictions. By thus setting himself against the source of his own being, man puts himself in contradiction with himself, his fellow-man and the world.

Because man is in this state of contradiction, he is also in a state of bondage. He is no longer free, but is confronted and limited at every turn by hostile forces which are too strong for him. The power of evil in the world around him, the power of sin in his own soul, and finally the power of death to put an end to his life, all combine to rob him of his freedom. And no power of his is enough to overcome these hostile powers and free him. The nature of this bondage, and the reasons for it, will be more fully examined in the next chapter.

II

To man thus in bondage and in self-contradiction, the message of salvation is sent. Salvation means that man is released from this bondage, and that the contradictions of which we have spoken are overcome. The Greek word which we translate as 'save' means 'to make whole'. It comes from the the same root as the Sanskrit *Sarva*. It means 'wholeness'. It means the healing of that which is wounded, the mending of that which is broken, the setting free of that which is bound.

Salvation is the fulfilling of God's original purpose in creation. When God created the world and mankind, it was His purpose that mankind should be one family bound to Him and to one another in love, and that the world should be a fit home for His children. It was His purpose that men should live in the knowledge and love of God, in obedience to Him, and in fellowship with one another. We shall see in the next chapter how sin came in and marred that original plan, and how God has acted to overcome sin, to deliver man from its bondage and to make him whole again.

That wholeness is salvation. It is spoken of in many ways in the Scriptures, by means of pictures and symbols. All nations and tribes and people shall be gathered together in one fellowship to worship God; all war and hatred shall cease; there shall be no more sorrow nor sighing; death itself shall be done away; even the wild creatures shall learn to live at peace—the wolf with the lamb and the bear with the ox; all the kingdoms of this world will become the kingdom of God; God Himself shall dwell with them and be their God; all the glory and honour of the nations shall be gathered into God's holy city, and nothing unclean or impure shall ever enter. It is in such words that the Bible describes to us the fulfilment of God's saving purpose. All mankind shall live together in one holy family, as children of one Father, in a new-created earth and heaven. That is salvation. Because we have received the earnest and first-fruits of it, we long for its completion. We know something of salvation now, because God has given us the earnest of it; we shall not know it fully until He has completed what He has begun.

II

WHAT IS SIN?

1. HOW DID IT ENTER THE WORLD?

I F we ask 'What is sin' we can answer the question very shortly by saying, 'Sin is disobedience to God'. It will help us most to understand the nature of sin if we study carefully what is told in the early chapters of Genesis about the way in which sin entered into human life.

(a) God created man in His own image[1]

All will agree that this is one of the fundamental texts of the Bible. Let us consider it somewhat closely. What is meant by 'The Image of God'? It is obvious that we do not mean that man's outward appearance is the same as God's. God has no outward appearance. God is Spirit; man is spirit and body. But it is noteworthy that the Scripture does not say that God created man's spirit in the image of His own Spirit, but simply that God created man in His own image. 'Male and female created he them.' But what is meant by 'in his image'?

The image of a king's head on a coin is part of the coin and cannot be separated from it. Even if the king dies, the image remains on the coin. But there is another kind of image. On a still and cloudless night we may see the image of the moon in the water of a lake. So long as the water is

[1] Gen. 1.26-27.

unruffled by wind, and the moon not covered by cloud, the image will shine out clear and beautiful. But if a cloud comes between the moon and the earth, the image will disappear or if the water is ruffled by wind, the image will be scattered and distorted. Thus the image of the moon in the water does not belong to the water in the same way that the image of the king on the coin belongs to the coin. The image depends upon a certain relation between the moon and the water. If this relation is broken, the image is distorted or lost.[2]

This parable will give us some help in understanding the image of God in man. It is more like the image in the water than the image on the coin. It depends for its existence upon a relation between God and man. The difference between man and every other creature is that man's manhood consists in his relation with God. A dog's dogginess is in itself. But man's humanity is not in himself; it is in the relation between himself and God. If that is destroyed, he ceases to be human and becomes a brute. Man's humanity consists in living in a relation of loving trust and obedience towards God, and in God's love of him. When man turns away from God, the image is distorted and spoiled; if God were to turn away from man, the image of God would be completely lost and man would no longer be human.

Thus the nature of man is that he was made in love, by love, for love. Love is the source and end of his being. Therefore man cannot live alone. For this reason, in the very same verse in which the Scripture tells us that God created man in His own image, it goes on to say 'male and female created he them'. When God created man He did not create an individual; He created man-and-woman. For God is not an individual; God is personal but He is not a

[2] I am indebted to Dr D. T. Niles for this illustration.

person. He is a Trinity, Father, Son and Holy Spirit, one God; one personal being in whom love is perfect and complete because love is both given and received. The Father loves the Son and the Son loves the Father, in the unity of the Holy Spirit. When we say 'God is Love', we mean that the fulness of love exists in God. But fulness of love only exists where love is both given and received. Fulness of love cannot exist in an individual. Therefore also when God created man in His own image, He created him male and female. The image of God is not seen in an individual man, but in man-and-woman bound together in love. Thus God has placed in the very constitution of man the need for and the possibility of love.

We are now able to see clearly what it means that God created man in His own image. It means that man's essential nature is to be found in a reflecting of God's love.

Man's existence is in the relationship of love to God and love to other human beings. We shall see later how this image has become distorted because man has used the possibility of love for the purpose of self-love.

(b) God gave the world which He had created to man to enjoy, but He placed a limit[3]

According to the story of the Bible, God placed all His wonderful creation at the disposal of man, and bade him enjoy it. He made man a sort of steward of His possessions. And we know that man has exercised this privilege in a remarkable way. He has turned trees, vegetables, beasts, birds, fishes to his use. He has exploited the resources of earth and sea and sky, of fire and lightning, and of the atom itself. He has endeavoured to subdue all things to his needs, and to-day man is even making plans to fly to the moon and the planets and make his power felt there.

[3] Gen. 2.7-17.

In fact man is tempted to believe that his power is infinite, and that there is no limit to what he can do.

But there is a limit. 'The Lord God commanded the man, saying, Of every tree of the garden thou mayest freely eat: but of the tree of the knowledge of good and evil thou shalt not eat of it: for in the day that thou eatest thereof thou shalt surely die.'[4] God has given man a very large measure of independence. But it is not a complete independence. If it were a complete independence, it would not be compatible with man's creation in His image. Because man's essential nature is that he was created in love for love, he cannot be completely independent; for love means both independence and dependence. If man could completely turn his back upon God, and become completely independent of Him, he would no longer be man. His existence is in his reflecting of the love of God.

Therefore the true knowledge of good and evil can only be given to man when he seeks it from God. However great be his power he can only know good and evil when he humbly seeks that knowledge from God his maker. With the independence God gave him, man has even learned to harness the power of the atom for his use; but because he seeks to have the determination of good and evil in his own power, and does not humbly seek it from God, this very power threatens to destroy him in frightful war.

(c) Man, wishing to be like God, transgresses that limit and falls into sin[5]

Man is made in the image of God; but he is not God. This situation provides the opportunity for temptation and sin. Temptation begins with distrust of God's goodness. The tempter suggests to Eve, very subtly, that God

[4] Gen. 2.16-17. [5] Gen. 3.1-6.

ought to have given to man the complete freedom to eat
of every tree. He suggests that the limit which God has
placed upon man shows that there is some lack in the love
of God. That distrust is the beginning of temptation.
Where there is perfect trust in God's fatherly goodness,
there can be no temptation. Unbelief is the beginning of
sin. Unbelief, in fact, is the very root and basis of sin.

Having sown the seed of unbelief in the heart of the
woman, the tempter now puts into her mind a new
suggestion: 'Ye shall be as God'.[6] When man ceases to
trust God completely, the next step is that he wants to
be God himself. He wants to be able to rule his own life,
to foresee the future, to determine what is good and what
is evil, to judge others, to be the centre of the world. That
is sin full-grown. Sin means that each man wants to be
the centre of the world, that he regards his own good as
more important than anything else; in other words, sin
means that each man wants to be God. Instead of loving
God with all his heart and soul and mind and strength he
loves himself. He gives to himself the honour which ought
to be given to God.

Thus we see how the possibility of sin arises from the
fact that man is created in the image of God. His true life
consists in loving faith towards God, acknowledging God
as the true centre of all things, trusting Him and obeying
Him. But just because man is created by God in His own
image, with the power to know and love God, he is
tempted to put himself in the place of God, to love himself instead of God. That is sin.

If we are to understand what salvation is, it is very
important for us to understand this point: that the essence
of sin is unbelief, and the opposite of sin is faith. We often
think that the opposite of sin is righteousness, but accord-

[6] Gen. 3.5.

ing to the teaching of the Bible the true opposite of sin is faith. If we understand this, we shall be able to understand the salvation which has been accomplished for us in Christ.

(d) As the result of his disobedience, man is driven from the presence of God and comes under a curse[7]

Because man has violated the nature which God gave him, and transgressed the limit which God placed for him, the unity and harmony of his life is at once utterly destroyed. This is seen in four principal ways:

1. There is disharmony within man himself. Firstly he becomes ashamed of his own body, and especially of its sexual organs, and tries to hide the nakedness of the body. Secondly he becomes ashamed of his own actions and tries to make excuses by blaming others (vv. 12-13). Thus man is no longer a unity. He is divided against himself, the spirit against the body, and the conscience against the self. Henceforth there will be warfare within man himself.

2. There is disharmony between man and nature. Man can no longer be simply at home in the natural world. The earth, the plants, and the beasts will no longer be his friends; he will have to fight with them to earn his bread (vv. 17-19). The natural processes of child-birth will be full of pain instead of pure joy (v. 16). In his heart he will always carry the memory of paradise, the memory of a time when the world was a garden in which he was at home; but henceforth he will not be able to return to it (vv. 23-24).

3. There is disharmony between man and man. Because man has sought to make himself the centre of the world, jealousy, hatred, and mutual strife will become the law of his life. It will be no longer natural for brothers to live

[7] Gen. 3.7-4.15.

together in love and co-operation. Brother will envy brother and slay him and will deny his brotherly responsibility, and the whole earth will become full of strife and death.[8]

4. Above all there is disharmony between man and God. When God calls man no longer runs to him with joy, as a child to its father. On the contrary, man is afraid of God's voice and hides himself.[9] Man becomes the enemy of God, knowing that he can never escape from God, and yet trying to evade Him. The voice of God fills him with terror. The law of God, which is love, is no longer the law of his own life; it becomes a commandment threatening him, because he knows that he does not keep it. Henceforth the story of the human race will be the story of God's long and patient search for man, who pretends that he is seeking God, but in truth is all the time running away from Him, and hiding himself from Him.

What is given to us in these chapters of Genesis is not geography or science or history. It is the truth about man expressed in pictures—the truth of his creation, of his nature, and of his sin. There are many other things that we can learn about the beginning of the human race, about the nature of the world, and about the history of man. For these we study the sciences of history, biology, astronomy, etc. What God had given to us in the Bible is the revelation of the nature which God has given to man, of the manner in which sin has corrupted that nature, and of the salvation which God has provided for us.

[8] Gen. 4.1-15.   [9] Gen. 3.9-10.

III

WHAT IS SIN?

2. THE NATURE OF SIN

FROM the reading of the Bible we learn to understand what is the essential nature of sin. In what has already been said certain things have been made clear about the nature of sin. Sin is a corruption of the nature of man due to the fact that he has become separated, alienated, turned away from God. Now we must try to understand more fully the nature of sin.

(a) Sin is a corruption of the very centre of human nature

Some people speak of sin as if it meant only the mistakes we make. Such people argue in the following way: Even a good man will sometimes make mistakes. Though his intentions are good, he will sometimes fall, through ignorance or through the weakness of human nature. At heart he is good, but he is not always able to live up to his own good intentions. This being so, we ought not to condemn him too severely, or to call him a sinner. We must hope that by education and character-building we can help him to overcome his faults. In fact at heart most men, or perhaps all men, are really good. They do make mistakes, but these mistakes can be overcome by good training. In order to achieve this we ought not to call men sinners, but to encourage them and give them confidence in themselves in order to bring out the best in them.

But Jesus did not look at the matter in this way. He said: 'A good tree cannot bring forth evil fruit, neither can a corrupt tree bring forth good fruit.'[1] It is not sufficient to say about our bad deeds and words that they are 'mistakes'; we have to ask 'Where do they come from?' And the answer can only be, 'They come from within, they come out of my own heart and mind'. Jesus emphasizes this truth again and again in different ways. 'The good man out of the good treasure of his heart bringeth forth good things, and the evil man out of his evil treasure bringeth forth evil things. And I say unto you, that every idle word that men shall speak, they shall give an account thereof in the day of judgment.'[2] And again He says: 'From within, out of the heart of men proceed evil thoughts, fornications, thefts, murders, adulteries, covetings, wickednesses, deceit, lasciviousness, an evil eye, railing, pride, foolishness; all these evil things proceed from within and defile the man.'[3]

Evil deeds and words are only the outward symptoms; the disease itself is an evil heart. That is sin, not just 'mistakes' but a heart and mind alienated from good and seeking evil. Education, training, character-building, can do much to keep the evil heart in check; but they cannot remove it, and its evil nature will come out in other ways. Sin is something which is seated at the very centre of the human personality. It is a corruption of the heart and soul of man.

This means that sin is not primarily a matter of the body. Many philosophers have taught that it was. The ancient Greeks taught that the soul of man was good, a spark of God's nature, but that it was imprisoned in the body and therefore prevented from fulfilling its divine nature. They regarded the body as evil, and therefore the

[1] Matt. 7.18.   [2] Matt. 12.35-36.   [3] Mark 7.21-23.

centre of their teaching about purification was teaching about how to overcome the lusts of the body. This sort of teaching is also common in India. Many people when they say 'sin' mean primarily those sins which arise from bodily lusts. But the Bible teaches that the root of sin is not in the body but in the mind and soul. The most terrible sins are spiritual sins—unbelief, pride, self-righteousness. In the New Testament we find that it was not the people ordinarily called 'sinners', but the religious leaders, those who were called 'righteous' who took the lead in murdering the Son of God. This is because the essence of sin is spiritual. Sin corrupts the whole of man—body, mind and soul. But the root of sin is in the very centre of man's nature—in his mind and soul.

(b) The root of sin is unbelief

We have already seen that, in the Genesis story, the beginning of sin is distrust of God. God is the source from which all that exists derives its being. He is the love by which all the world is sustained. He has made man in His own image, so that man might not only live by that love (as all created things do), but also know that love and respond to it with answering love. Man is truly man when he lives by trusting and loving God. Sin is a contradiction of the very essence of man's being; it is man turning away from God, distrusting Him, withholding love from Him.

Because man is made in God's image, that is, made in order to know and love God, he may contradict his own nature but he cannot destroy it. If he does not love and trust God, he must love and trust something else. Therefore he loves himself. So sin comes to mean self-love. The love of man, which should reach out to grasp the love of God, becomes turned inwards to man himself. Instead of glorifying God, he seeks to glorify himself. Instead of rejoicing to do God's will, he wants to do his own will. Instead of trusting God, relying upon Him for everything which he needs, he relies upon himself. Instead of bowing before God's judgment, he tries to become judge himself, judging other men's hearts and behaving as though he were himself God. In other words, sin means that man, instead of finding the centre of his life in God, tries to make himself the centre of the world.

When once this terrible corruption has been introduced into human nature, it goes on working and developing, and producing more and more corruption. The root-sin of unbelief drives man deeper into sin. In the rest of this chapter we shall see some of the ways in which this happens.

(c) Unbelief, anxiety, and the lie

Unbelief means that man turns from the true God to a false God—to himself. He behaves as though he were the centre of the world, as though his own good were the most important thing in the world, as though other people existed in order to serve his own ends. But of course this behaviour is based on a lie. Man is not the centre of the world; God is. In his deepest heart man knows that this is a lie. He knows that he is not the centre of the world; he knows that he cannot himself control the world, or even control the events of one day in his own life. He is threatened in all sorts of ways—threatened by the natural calamities that may come to any man, such as sickness, bereavement, unemployment or other accident, threatened by the claims of other men who also behave as if they were the centres of the world and seek to override and exploit him, threatened above all by death. All these things make him anxious. And in order to overcome his anxiety he must still more assert himself as if he were the controller of events. He tries to safeguard himself in all sorts of ways, and to increase his power to control his environment, and the people around him. But the more he does this, the more anxious he becomes. The more he accumulates wealth to safeguard himself, the more he fears its loss. The more he tries to become the leader among his fellow-men, the more afraid he becomes of the rivalry of others. The more he tries to make himself secure in this life, the more he is afraid of death. The more he fears, the more he tries to shut out the truth, and the more he shuts out the truth the more he fears. The more he succeeds, the more he is blinded to the truth. Thus the lie in his heart eventually creates a deep dishonesty in his whole conduct. Even his conscience becomes corrupted, and he does evil things believing that they are good. Thus the Jewish church leaders crucified Christ, believing that they were serving God. This is why Jesus had to speak such terrible words to them in order to make them understand that, although they said 'we see', they were really blind.[4] Sin creates blindness, but those who are thus blinded do not know that they are blind. As St Paul says: 'They hold down the truth in unrighteousness.'[5]

(d) Idolatry

In the first chapter of Romans, verses 18 to the end, St Paul describes in a very terrible way the progressive corruption which is created by unbelief. He first speaks of the dishonesty which it produces—'holding down the truth in unrighteousness'. Then he says that this causes men to 'change the glory of the incorruptible God for the likeness of an image of corruptible man and of birds, and four-footed beasts, and creeping things'.[6] He is speaking here of the idolatry which the Christians of the first cen-

[4] John 9.39-41.   [5] Rom. 1.18.   [6] Rom. 1.22f.

tury saw all around them and with which we are familiar in India. But there are also many other kinds of idolatry, of which we shall speak in a moment. Why does Paul speak of idolatry as the result of unbelief? We have seen that at the heart of man's sin there is a lie. Man is not the centre of the world, he knows that he is not. Because he was made by God for God, his heart still longs for something outside himself which he can trust and serve. But having turned away from the living God he seeks this among the created things, or among the works of his own hands. He wants to have something which he can see, or touch, or understand, so that he can be sure. The anxiety of which we have spoken in the previous paragraph drives him to seek this security against all the mysterious evils of the world and against death itself. Much of what we call 'religion' is an attempt to find this security. But many things which are not usually called 'religious' have the same character. The most terrible form of idolatry in modern Europe has been nationalism. Millions of people who have lost faith in God have been driven to seek in their nation a security against the perils of life. Men who as individuals know that they are weak and fallible and mortal, try to find a sense of strength and security in their nation which seems to be strong and enduring. Sometimes there has been a conscious deification of the State, as in the case of Germany in the time of Hitler. More often this idolatry is hidden in the heart and not openly confessed.

(e) Sensuality and lust

In the first chapter of Romans, St Paul goes on to say that because men 'exchanged the truth of God for a lie, and worshipped and served the creature rather than the Creator', therefore God gave them up to lust, sensuality, and uncleanness (vv. 24-27). When we put the created thing in the place of the Creator, this is what happens. Man is made for God, who is infinite; therefore man's desires are infinite and no finite thing can satisfy them. When man turns away from God and seeks to satisfy himself with created things they do not satisfy him. Because his desire is infinite, he tries to get more and more of the same thing. If a man has found the satisfaction of all his desires in God, he will receive from God's hands all the natural things which God has created—food, drink, sexual pleasure, possessions, etc. He will use them with thanksgiving, according to God's laws, and will be thankful to God. But if he has not found satisfaction in God, he will seek it in these things, and then he will become a glutton, a drunkard, a sensualist, a miser. This is one of the great differences between a man and an animal.

Because an animal is not made in the image of God, its desires are limited; if it is given sufficient food, space, and opportunity for reproduction, it will be satisfied. But because man is created in the image of God, his desires are unlimited and unless he finds satisfaction for them in God, he will never be satisfied with created things and will want more and more of them. This is why St Paul says that covetousness is idolatry.[7] When we covet, we are putting some created thing in the place which only God can fill. We are saying 'If only I had that thing, that money, that social position, that work, that house, I should be happy'. But the truth is that we should not. Only God can make us happy. It is when we do not know this that we become victims of our own lust and fall into the snares of sensuality. St Augustine truly prayed: 'Lord, thou hast made us for Thyself and our hearts are restless

[7] Col. 3.5.

till they find rest in Thee.' Sensuality is the attempt to satisfy an infinite desire with finite goods. It ends in despair and death. We see now that sensuality and lust are not the root of sin, but its fruit.

(f) Envy, strife and murder

St Paul ends this terrible chapter by showing that the final fruit of sin is that men become 'full of envy, murder, strife, deceit, malignity; whisperers, backbiters, hateful to God, insolent, haughty, boastful, inventors of evil things, disobedient to parents, without understanding, covenant-breakers, without natural affection, unmerciful.'[8] This is a terrible picture, but it is a true one. The final result of sin is that human brotherhood is destroyed, the natural ties that bind men one to another are broken, and man becomes inhuman. We have seen that happen in the world. Of course this is not the whole truth. God is always working in the world to prevent sin from utterly destroying the human race. By the institution of the State He holds in check the worst forms of evil. By the institution of the family He provides a very strong natural bond to draw men, women, and children into a single fellowship. By the necessary conditions of man's economic life He provides incentives which draw men together in co-operation. In other ways too He holds in check the destructive power of sin. And yet this terrible power is all the time at work in the world, causing nation to fight against nation, breaking up the unity of nations, of tribes, and of families and causing men to be their own enemies and to destroy their own selves in all kinds of senseless folly. All these things are the fruits of sin, its outward symptoms. If we are to understand how this terrible power can be overcome, we must understand that the root

[8] Rom. 1.29-31.

is not in these things, but in unbelief, the unbelief which causes man to turn away from God his Creator. This chapter of St Paul has shown us how from this root comes first anxiety, then deceit, then false worship, then lust and sensuality, and finally envy, strife, and murder. This is the terrible fruit that grows from the seed of unbelief.

IV

THE SITUATION WHICH SIN HAS PRODUCED

(a) *The results of sin are real and terrible*

IF we are to understand the situation which sin produces we can best begin by looking at two passages in the Bible. At the beginning of Genesis we read that God created all things simply by His Word.

When He said: 'Let there be light', there was light. There is here no obstacle for Him to overcome. He does not require to struggle with difficult material, as a carpenter must struggle to shape his wood, or a writer must struggle to find the right words, or a statesman must struggle to carry his plans into effect. The Word of God is enough to create the heavens and the earth and all that is in them, to rule the stars and to check the raging of the seas.[1] But now look at another picture: the Son of God, the Word of God made flesh, kneels in the garden of Gethsemane. He wrestles in prayer. His sweat falls like great drops of blood. He cries out in an agony: 'Not my will, but thine be done'. That is what it costs God to deal with man's sin. To create the heavens and the earth costs Him no labour, no anguish; to take away the sin of the world costs Him His own life-blood.

Sin is not a mere illusion which could be cleared away by mere illumination. It is not like an entry in a book which could simply be deleted, a debt which can easily

[1] Cf. Pss. 93, 104 and many others.

32

be remitted. It creates a situation which is real and terrible not only for men, but also for God. In this respect the Hindu doctrine of *Karma* is one which has an important element of truth. That doctrine is not wholly true, for it teaches that every man must bear his own *Karma*, whereas the truth is that God has bound us up together in such a way that we may and must bear one another's *Karma*. A son bears the weight of his father's sin, and a mother of her son's. It is because God has made us so that it was possible for the Son of Man to bear the *Karma* of mankind. But the doctrine of *Karma* is true when it teaches that man's sin produces a result which cannot be evaded, or ignored, but must be expiated and overcome. 'Whatsoever a man soweth that shall he also reap.'[2] God is not mocked; we cannot play with Him. Life is not a children's game of 'make-believe'. Real issues are at stake, real decisions are made. It is a fatal illusion to think that all roads lead to the same end. On the contrary, there is a road that leads to life and a road that leads to death. The wages of sin is death—that is a truth which every man must learn sooner or later.

We have already seen some of the results of sin. We have seen that sin produces an alienation between man and God, between man and himself, between man and the natural world, and between man and his neighbour. The first and fundamental alienation is between man and God, the cutting off of man from the source and centre of his being. The result of that is a division within man himself, so that he becomes a divided being—flesh against spirit, conscience against natural desire. At the same time he becomes alienated from the natural world about him. He is no longer one with it, but finds it to be his enemy. And his own brother becomes his enemy whom he envies or

[2] Gal. 6.7.

B

fears. We have also seen that the effect of sin is to blind man to the truth. Because sin is based upon a lie it breeds lies. It corrupts man's own conscience, so that he is blind to the truth, does evil while persuading himself that it is good, and finally becomes the murderer of the Son of God. All these things are real facts which have to be dealt with. Neither God nor man can act as though they did not exist.

(b) Guilt and responsibility

The next thing which we have to notice about the situation which sin produces is that it is something which even God cannot remove apart from man, because the centre of the problem is man's guilt and responsibility. We often speak of sin as uncleanness, and that is a natural metaphor. But we must remember that there is a very great difference between sin and uncleanness. If a child's face is dirty, its mother can wipe the dirt off its face even while it sleeps. But sin cannot be wiped out of the soul like that. Even God cannot do so. When the Psalmist asks God: 'Wash me throughly from mine iniquity and cleanse me from my sin', it is because he can also say 'I acknowledge my transgressions, and my sin is ever before me'.[3] Sin can never be removed until the sinner acknowledges it, confesses it, and repudiates it. He must first acknowledge it (v. 3). Then he must confess it to God: 'Against thee, thee only, have I sinned and done that which is evil in thy sight' (v. 4). And finally he must utterly repudiate it, putting it away from him and disowning it.

This point needs to be strongly stressed. As we have seen in discussion of the Genesis story, one of the first effects of sin is that the sinner tries to deny his own responsibility. Every sinner is tempted to add to his sin

[3] Ps. 51.2-3.

by making excuses. Adam blames Eve, and Eve blames the serpent. For every sin men find some sort of excuse—their troubles, their bad environment, or their *Karma*. Of course there is often some sort of truth in these excuses. There are circumstances which create a temptation to sin. We shall speak about that in the next section. But nevertheless the excuse is false. It is true that Eve tempted Adam, but he could have said 'No'.

It is true that when we are in trouble there is a very strong temptation to escape by lying or thieving or other forms of sin. But temptation is not compulsion. We have the power to say 'No'. Therefore if we say 'Yes' we are responsible. This responsibility is, as we have seen, the very essence of man's nature as God has created him. God has scores of creatures who do all their actions according to the compulsion of nature. They act as they are led to act by hunger, fear, herd instinct, etc. They are not responsible. But man has been created in the image of God, with the freedom which is proper to a responsible person, in order that he may freely and voluntarily love and serve God. This responsibility is the very essence of human nature. It is because he has this freedom that man is able to sin. Sin is impossible for animals; it is the misuse of the specifically human gift of freedom. Whatever temptations I may have had to sin, and however many other people have been guilty of the same sin, I and I alone am responsible for my sin. And my sin can only be put away when I acknowledge it, accept my responsibility, and confess it. Even God cannot do that for me apart from my will.

And yet my repentance is not itself enough to put away my sin. My sin has started a train of consequences which my repentance cannot stop. Judas bitterly repented of his betrayal of Jesus, but that did not stop the crucifixion. If I have spoken an evil word, or passed on a slander, I may repent of it sincerely; but the slander will go on spreading from mouth to mouth and poisoning men's minds long afterwards. When I think about my sin, it is not enough that I should think only of my own repentance and forgiveness. I have to think of the infinite consequence of my sin in the lives of other people, of the injury done to many whom (perhaps) I have never known. And, above all, I have to think of what my sin means to God. 'Against thee, thee only have I sinned.' My sin is a deliberate wounding of the loving heart of God. Even my complete repentance cannot undo that fact. Sin is not put away unless all these terrible consequences are somehow dealt with.

(c) *Corporate guilt, original sin, and temptation*

Hitherto we have been thinking about sin in individual terms—as the sin of a single man. But our human life is lived in groups—families, tribes, nations, societies. We do not live alone, and we do not sin alone. As nations and societies we have a joint responsibiliity for many grievous sins. These are the sins of which we are usually unconscious. If I commit a sin which is contrary to the general public opinion round me—for example, breaking into a house and stealing jewels—public opinion will condemn me, and my conscience will probably condemn me very severely. If I commit the same sin of theft in a way which is very common (for example, by drawing travelling allowance in excess of my actual expenses) my conscience will perhaps not condemn me so severely. But I am equally guilty. And there are other sins so common that we hardly think of them as sins—for instance, spreading infectious diseases by unhygienic habits. These also bring their harvest of disease and death and sorrow, and for this I am responsible. But in many of these things we cannot fix the whole responsibility on any one person. The whole society is corporately responsible. Thus we have to use the concept of 'corporate guilt'. Many of the most terrible forms of sin are those which come under this heading—not the sins which individuals commit and which all good men condemn, but the sins in which all men are involved and about which only very few men feel a sense of guilt and responsibility. Thus for seventeen or eighteen centuries after Christ the custom of slavery was continued in Christian countries, and no one thought that it was wrong. But it was wrong, and it brought forth the harvest of sorrow, suffering, and death which sin always brings. Society was corporately guilty. Only in the eighteenth and nineteenth centuries men began to see that it was wrong, and to rouse others to a sense of guilt, so that the sinful practice could be stopped.

We have to apply this concept of corporate guilt to the whole human race. Just as families, nations and societies are corporately guilty of many sins, so the human race as a whole is corporately guilty of sin against God. St. Paul speaks much about this especially in Romans 5.12-21. This is how he interprets the story of the Fall in Genesis chapter 3. The whole human race is under the power of sin and death, guilty and under the wrath of God. Even when men are not conscious of any sin, when they do not think they are guilty, yet they are part of this whole guilty human race. In Romans 5.13-14 and more fully in ch. 7, he shows that it was the work of the Law to bring men to a knowledge of their guilt. Nevertheless even before the giving of the Law, when men lacked knowledge of their guilt, they were still guilty and under the reign of death. The first sin started a train of sins that goes on right through the human race. Even though each of us is responsible for his own sin, nevertheless there is a corporate sin in which we share even before we commit actual deeds. Even the new-born babe does not start with an equal freedom to do good or evil. It does not start like a balance evenly held, but with one side heavily weighed down. It is easier for it to do evil than to do good, easier to seek good things for itself than to seek them for others. Even in its own nature there is a bias towards evil. And as it grows up it finds itself in an environment which has been shaped by human sin, and which therefore provides many more incentives towards evil. Every human being thus inherits a nature which is already tainted by sin, and every man also commits sins for which he is individually responsible. Theologians describe these two things by using the terms 'original sin' and 'actual sin'. As we have repeatedly seen, sin is a corruption of the very nature of man himself, and is a deeper and more serious thing than simply his sinful acts. Salvation must mean the giving of a new nature to man, so that he not only does good but is good. It is that new nature which Christ gives to those who believe in Him. He speaks of it in many ways—of being born again, of dying in order to live, of becoming children of God. Nothing less than the giving of a new human nature will solve the problem of sin. Jesus saves us from sin by giving us His own new human nature, making us members in His body, branches in Him the True Vine. He is thus described by St Paul as the 'last Adam', the beginning of a new human race freed from the law of sin and living under the law of grace.[4]

It is because of this fallen human nature which we all inherit, that temptation has such power. Before every actual sin, there is always the temptation to sin. The suggestion of evil is present before the evil act. Where

[4] Rom. 5.12-21; I Cor. 15.42-45.

does this suggestion come from? Usually we can trace the source from which it came—the evil advice of another person, the bad example of others, the suggestion of books we have read or pictures we have seen. When a man allows his mind to be filled with evil thoughts through conversation, reading, or seeing pictures, it is certain that when he is in difficulties evil suggestions will come to him as temptations. His own previous sins will increase the strength of the temptation to sin. But this does not fully answer the question. If my temptation comes from the previous sin of myself or others, from the original sin which I inherit, where did the first temptation come from? The Bible story tells that it was the serpent who tempted Eve, and it has been common to identify the serpent with Satan—although the Bible does not say this. Certainly the Bible teaches that there is an evil power outside of man, tempting man to sin—the power of Satan. If we press the question still further and ask—how did Satan first sin, we have no clear answer. We know that God created all things good, and that Satan must therefore have been originally good. It is an ancient belief of the Church that Satan was an angel who fell through pride. But even when we have said this, we have not 'explained' the origin of evil. When we get to the bottom of this dark mystery we must say: 'We do not know'. There are many things about our life of which we must say 'We do not know' and this is one of them. Sin is a dark and terrible mystery. We can understand something, but at the bottom there is a mystery which we cannot penetrate. When the disciples of Jesus asked Him 'Did this man sin, or his father, that he should be born blind?' Jesus did not answer the question but said that the works of God were to be made manifest in him, and immediately healed him.[5] God

[5] John 9.1-7.

has not shown us everything about the origin of evil; but
He has shown us His own saving work by which evil is
overcome. It is to that that we have to pay attention.

(d) Man cannot save himself from sin

We have seen that sin is a corruption of the very heart
of man's nature, and that this corruption has spread
through the whole human race. There is no part of the
human race which is free from sin and therefore able to
lift up the rest. There is no part of man's nature which is
free from sin and able to redeem man himself. The reason
for this will be clear from what has already been said. The
centre of man's nature is the will, and it is the will itself
which is turned away from God. Even when man desires
to be free from sin, to be reconciled with God, to be holy
as God is holy, that desire is corrupted by the self-seeking
which is the heart of sin. Man desires these things for
himself; the result of that desire is to be seen in great
religious systems, in systems of morality, in all kinds of
human ideals and movements for realizing them. But all
these things become themselves the vehicles of man's
pride and self-seeking. We see that most clearly in the
New Testament, where the religious and ethical leaders,
the priests, scribes, teachers of the law, and pharisees,
were those who became the murderers of Jesus. Man's
effort to save himself becomes the most terrible form of
his sin. Self-righteousness is the most terrible contradiction of the love of God.

This is the position of sinful man. He knows—at least
in some degree—that he is a sinner, because God's law
has been given to him in his conscience and in the words
of the great religious teachers and prophets. But he cannot
save himself from his sin. No one can save him except
God, against whom he has sinned. Everything depends

upon the answer to this question: 'Does God save man from his sin?'

But we have to ask: 'How can God save man from his sin?' We have already seen that the essence of the problem of sin is that man is responsible, and that he cannot be freed from his sins by an act of almighty power from outside. Even God cannot remove man's sins as a mother removes the dirt from her child's face. Sin is a corruption of the will of man, and can only be removed by a change in the will of man. How can this change be brought about? God, the Creator of heaven and earth, is a God of holy love. That is the foundation upon which the whole creation rests. Because He is holy love, He repels and resists sin. If He did not do so, the whole creation would be destroyed by sin. The reason why this does not happen is that God's wrath meets and resists sin. If this did not happen, God would not be God. In an earlier section we studied the first chapter of the Epistle to Romans, and saw how the corruption of sin leads stage by stage to the total breaking up of human society. If we look again at the chapter, we shall see that Paul speaks of this as 'the wrath of God' (v. 18, see also vv. 24 and 28). This is not something which works automatically like a machine. It is because God is God that He resists sin, punishes it, and causes it to end in destruction and death. If God ceased to do this, He would not be God, and the world would be utterly destroyed.

When men speak of forgiveness, they sometimes speak as though they wished God simply to treat sin as if it was not sin, to accept it and let it pass. That would be the end of all things. There is only right because God upholds it; there is only truth because God upholds it. If God were to treat wrong as though it were right, and lies as though they were truth, that would be the end of all things.

God's wrath is revealed from heaven, says St Paul, against all the unrighteousness of men. If that were not so, there would be no righteousness.

But God's wrath does not bring salvation. It does not bring reconciliation between man and God, nor does it give to men a new nature free from sin. Unless God's mercy and grace are also stirred to save, there can be no salvation. But how can mercy and grace go together with wrath? How can God save the sinner while at the same time resisting and destroying his sin? That is the terrible problem which sin creates. Has God given the answer to it?

The Gospel is the good news that He has done so, that mercy has triumphed over wrath, that there is a way for sinful men to be reconciled with Holy God. We have now to tell the story of that victory.

V

THE PREPARATION FOR SALVATION

(a) The story of salvation the story of actual events

WE must begin by making it clear that we are going to talk about actual events which have happened in history. Salvation from sin is something which man cannot achieve for himself, and the way in which God has saved him is something which he could not imagine for himself. Our gospel is not the thoughts of men but the acts of God. The God who created all things, against whom man has rebelled, has done certain mighty deeds by which salvation is brought to the human race. It is only by attending to these events, learning to understand them, and believing in them, that we can be saved. Many people resent this very much. They do not want to have to depend upon particular events. They wish to have a religion which can be found by the student in his solitary study, or by the devotee in his solitary prayer. But God has not so dealt with us. Sin, as we have said before, is not an illusion which can be dispelled simply by knowledge of the truth. It is a terrible reality which could only be overcome by mighty acts of God. Therefore in order to be sharers in the salvation which God has given we have to pay attention to the things which He has done for our salvation. We shall be studying history.

(b) The election of a people

But we shall not be studying the whole history of the

43

human race. The sin is the sin of the whole human race, and the salvation is the salvation of the whole human race; but God's way of salvation works through the choosing of a particular people, and finally of one man of that people. So we have to study the history of God's chosen people, the Jews. The Jews were one of the small tribes who lived in the narrow strip of hill-country between the desert of Arabia and the Mediterranean Sea. They were for a long time slaves in Egypt. Then for a long time they were divided under different rulers, often fighting among themselves, often crushed by powerful enemies. For a few years they were under a single rule— in the reigns of David and Solomon. Then almost at once they were again divided into two kingdoms, often almost crushed by the surrounding peoples. After many struggles the northern kingdom was completely destroyed by Assyria and its people carried away as slaves. After another short period the southern kingdom was likewise destroyed by the Babylonian empire. Thereafter, except for a very brief period, the Jews were never free. They were under Persian, Greek, or Roman power, until at last the Romans came and utterly destroyed their city and brought their national life to an end. It was through this small, apparently insignificant people, that God was pleased to reveal His salvation.

There are many for whom this teaching is unwelcome. We are inclined to ask: 'Why should I study the history of this obscure and unattractive tribe? Why should I not study what God has done for my own people and my own land? Can I not find Him in these things?' As Naaman the Syrian Commander-in-Chief said, when he was told to wash in the river Jordan: 'Are not Abanah and Pharpar, the rivers of Damascus, better than all the waters of Israel? May I not wash in them and be clean?'

All of us in some degree feel this difficulty. But the fact remains that, as Jesus said: 'Salvation is from the Jews.'[1] We must admit that there is a mystery here. We cannot say why God should have chosen the Jews rather than any other people to be the means of salvation, just as we cannot understand why He should have chosen us and not others to be the witnesses to His gospel in India to-day. But if we reflect a little we can understand why He should work by this way of choosing. It is His purpose to create a new human race in which the divisions caused by sin are overcome, in which men are at one with God, with one another, and with themselves. This means that the salvation which He has prepared is not something for each individual separately but for the human race together. If He wished to deal with each human being separately, the proper way would be for Him to give the message of salvation to each man equally and separately, through reason, or conscience, or spiritual insight. In that case there would be no need for preaching, for everyone would know the truth for himself. But God's will is different. He desires to knit together into one holy family the whole race of men broken by sin. Therefore He chooses one man, one race, in order that through them others may be saved. Each one who has been reconciled to God has to be the means by which others are reconciled. Thus God's purpose is fulfilled by a visible earthly fellowship of men and women—beginning with those whom He has first chosen, and spreading out to others.

We can put the whole matter most simply in this way: God's nature is love, and salvation means being restored to life in the love of God and in love with His children. But love only exists in actual concrete human relationships. Love in general is nothing at all; true love means

[1] John 4.22.

care for real people—my brother, my fellow-worker, my
neighbour. We have to give and receive love in dealing
with actual men and women—not just those whom we
choose, but those whom God gives to us. So it is that the
centre of God's plan for salvation is an actual community
of men and women called by God for this purpose. They
are not called because they are better than others; nor are
they called because God wants to save them only. They
are called in order that through them God's love may
reach others, and all men be drawn together into one
reconciled fellowship.

(c) The preparation for Christ

The story of salvation begins when God calls a man to
leave home and people and to go out trusting in God
alone. 'Now the Lord said unto Abram, Get thee out of thy
country, and from thy kindred, and from thy father's
house, unto the land that I will show thee; and I will make
of thee a great nation, and I will bless thee and make thy
name great. . . . And in thee shall all the families of the
earth be blessed.'[2] And Abraham believed God and
obeyed.[3] God called a man, not just for himself, but for
the sake of all nations; and the man believed and obeyed
and 'went out, not knowing whither he went'.

There is not space here to re-tell the long story that
follows, how the seed of Abraham again and again forgot
the purpose of their calling, again and again denied God
and fell into slavery and ruin, and how God again and
again recalled them and held before them the still-
unfulfilled promise. The climax of the story comes when
God sends His own Son to be born of the chosen people,
and that people (through its anointed leader the high
priest) condemns Him and crucifies Him. We shall see how

[2] Gen. 12.1-3.   [3] See Heb. 11.8.

that event was the means by which salvation was finally accomplished. But first we must see how the long history of the Jewish people prepared for this consummation. In order to do so, we shall take three main strands in the story and show how they lead up to Jesus and His cross. The story of the Old Testament is the story of prophets, priests and kings. If we take these three great types of leader in the Old Testament story, we shall see how that story is the preparation for salvation through Jesus Christ.

1. *The Prophet.* The greatest figure in the Old Testament story is Moses, the prophet through whom God made known to His people His fundamental laws. And Moses was followed by a great line of men who carried forward the same work—Samuel, Elijah, Amos, Hosea, Isaiah, Jeremiah and many more. These men were raised up by God from time to time in order to re-call the people to the will of God, to show them the meaning of what God was doing in the world, to warn them of God's judgment against sinners, and to demand in God's name that God's people should walk in His ways. Their whole message may be summed up in the great words of the prophet Micah : 'Wherewith shall I come before the Lord; and bow myself before the High God? Shall I come before him with burnt offerings, with calves of a year old? Will the Lord be pleased with thousands of rams, or with ten thousands of rivers of oil? Shall I give my first-born for my transgression, the fruit of my body for the sin of my soul? He hath showed thee, O man, what is good; and what doth the Lord require of thee but to do justly, to love mercy, and to walk humbly with thy God?'[4] That is indeed God's will for man, and no kind of religion can be substituted for it. But who can say that he has fulfilled these requirements? The book of Leviticus summed up the whole of

[4] Mic. 6.6-8.

man's duty to his neighbour by saying: 'Thou shalt love thy neighbour as thyself.'[5] But what man can say truly: 'I love every man as I love myself'? And if I cannot say so, if I cannot fulfil the law of God, what is my position? Am I not damned? How shall I escape out of this position? That question presses harder and harder, the more seriously we take the will of God. The best among the Jews took the will of God very seriously and wanted to fulfil it completely. They made more and more careful rules to govern every part of life and they insisted that they should be completely kept. They believed that if the whole Law of God could be completely kept even for one day, the kingdom of God would come. But the effect of this was that they had to concentrate their attention more and more upon those parts of the Law of God which a man can completely keep. This means, in effect, the negative prohibitions of the Law, the ceremonial rules, rules regarding tithes, sacrifices, etc. All these things could be completely kept, and a man could say at the end of a day: 'I thank God that I am not as other men; I have fully kept the law.' That was the aim of the Pharisees, who were the strict Jews of the time of Christ.

We know the criticism which our Lord had to make of this kind of religion. He told them that they were fulfilling all the little matters of the Law, and forgetting all the great ones. 'Ye tithe mint and anise and cummin, and have left undone the weightier matters of the law, judgment and mercy and faith.'[6] They had shut out of view the great unfulfillable demands of the Law, in order to enjoy the self-righteousness which comes through fulfilling the lesser parts of the Law. Above all, because they were self-righteous they were loveless; and since love is the sum of the Law, they were in truth transgressors of the Law.

[5] Lev. 19.18.   [6] Matt. 23.23.

And because the coming of Jesus exposed their trans-gression; because in the light of Jesus all their righteous-ness was shown to be filthy rags, they hated Him and killed Him.

God had led His people through the witness of the prophets to a clearer and clearer understanding of His will. Until they knew what His will was, they could not be saved. But the knowledge of His will alone could not bring salvation. This is shown by the fact that those who were most zealous to fulfil God's Law were those who rejected the salvation which Christ brought. Therefore the true prophets always looked beyond their own message to a Coming One who would bring God's righteousness with Him. The last of the prophets was John the Baptist and he too pointed beyond his own message of repentance to the Lamb of God who would take away the sins of the world. Repentance, knowledge of God's will, obedience to it—these are all necessary; it was the work of the prophets to bring about these things. But these things cannot bring salvation. They point beyond themselves; they are wit-nesses to God's righteousness but they do not themselves produce God's righteousness. Only when God Himself became man, born under the Law and fulfilling the Law to the last limit, could the Law fulfil its work.[7] Thus the great line of prophets and law-givers, from Moses to John the Baptist, was a necessary preparation for the coming salvation, but could not itself produce salvation. That only God Himself could bring.

2. *The Priest.* Without obedience to God's Law there can be no salvation, but the Law does not bring us sal-vation because the sinfulness of our own heart causes us to break the Law. And yet man cannot live without God. But how shall sinful man live with God who is holy? That

[7] Gal. 4.4-5.

has always been part of the problem of religion, and it
has always been the business of priests to show the way
by which it may be solved. The work of the priest has
always been—in part at least—to look after the business
of sacrifice, prayer and ritual by which men stained by
sin may be able to have fellowship with God. And the Old
Testament is no exception. Throughout it we find that
men offer sacrifices and make prayers, and that there are
priests who act as mediators between God and sinful men.

When we look at this part of the Old Testament more
closely, we see that the system of sacrifices is not something which men have planned in order to propitiate God;
it is something which God has provided in order that men
may approach Him. And yet, at the same time, the sacrifices have to be offered by men as the condition of their
coming to God. This paradoxical character of forgiveness
is something which we shall have to speak about again.
Man cannot by any propitiation put himself right with
God; but neither can God by a mere act of omnipotence
wipe away man's sin. So the whole sacrificial system has
this double character—it is something provided by God
for man to offer to God. And between man and God stands
the priest, consecrated to bring men's sacrifices to God in
the way He has ordained.

The story of the development of the system of priesthood and sacrifice in the Old Testament is a long one for
which there is not space here. But one thing can be briefly
said. In the earliest days sacrifices were offered in every
place, and there were priests in every place to offer them.
They were generally happy occasions, times of rejoicing
and fellowship. We can see this from the books of Judges
and Samuel. But later on the situation changed. After the
reign of Josiah sacrifice was prohibited in any place except
Jerusalem. It became a much more restricted affair. The

more the sense of God's holiness was deepened, the more the sense of His distance from man was increased, and therefore the more narrow became the way of sacrifice. More emphasis was placed on the sin-offering and the guilt-offering. The ordinary man could only rarely offer sacrifice and the centre of the Temple—the Holy of Holies —was completely cut off from the ordinary worshipper. Only the high priest could enter it, and that only once a year, on the Day of Atonement. Moreover the sins for which the priest could offer sacrifice were only sins of ignorance. Deliberate sins ('sins done with a high hand') could not be expiated by sacrifice.

Thus the sacrificial system, which was intended to make it possible for sinful men to have fellowship with God, became more and more something which fenced up the way from man to God. The great mass of the people were excluded for most of their lives from its benefits. The sacrificial system could not do what it was intended to do. It could only be a sign and witness to the need of a way from man to God, but it could not provide that way. That way could only be provided when the Son of God Himself came, to be both Priest and Sacrifice. Just as the Epistles to the Romans and to the Galatians show how the work of law and prophets is fulfilled in Christ, so the Epistle to the Hebrews shows how the priesthood and the sacrificial system are fulfilled in Him. After having spoken in detail of the sacrifices of the Temple, the author says: 'that these gifts and sacrifices cannot, as touching the conscience, make the worshipper perfect, being only (with meats and drinks and diverse washings) carnal ordinances imposed until a time of reformation. But Christ, having come a high priest of the good things to come, through the greater and more perfect tabernacle not made with hands, that is to say not of this creation nor yet through the blood of goats and calves, but through his own blood, entered in once for all into the holy place, having obtained eternal redemption.'[8] He Himself, who is both God and Man, can alone provide the true sacrifice, the true way from man to God, the true mercy-seat where sinners may be accepted to God. He alone is the true High Priest. All human priesthood can only point to Him; it cannot itself accomplish what it intends to do.

3. *The King.* The Old Testament also tells the story of the search for true kingship, that is to say, for the true manner in which God's rule should be carried out in the life of an earthly community. From the beginning the Hebrews knew that in truth God alone is truly King. But how was God's Kingship to become effective in the life of a nation? That is the problem of all politics. At first they had no king and—as the Book of Judges says: 'Every man did that which was right in his own eyes.'[9] But the resulting chaos made men long for a king to give them permanent leadership. The first Book of Samuel records two different traditions about the beginning of the Kingship. According to one (I Sam. 8.7 ff.) the demand for a king was regarded as a rebellion against God. But in other places (e.g. 9.15-16) the calling and anointing of Saul to be king was an act of God's mercy done in order to save Israel out of its troubles. The whole story of kingship in the Old Testament continues to show this double character. David is portrayed as a true king after God's own heart; and yet even in David's reign, and much more in the reigns of his successors, the evils that arrive from earthly kingship are vividly brought out. For centuries men looked back to the reign of David as a golden age, and longed for the day when God would bring a king like him, a 'son of David' to the throne. Their longing for the

[8] Heb. 9.9-12   [9] Judg. 21.25.

coming of the kingdom of God was expressed in terms of a longing that a true son of David might come to the throne and might extend his blessed reign over the whole world.[10]

When the true son of David did come, this very expectation of an earthly kingship was one of the obstacles to His ministry. When men tried to force Him to become king, He hid Himself from them.[11] He had to prevent His disciples from acting as though His kingdom were an earthly kingdom.[12] He had to reject the temptation of the Devil to establish just such an earthly kingdom.[13]

For the truth is that earthly kingship, even at its best, can only be a sign and witness to the kingdom of God; it cannot itself bring in the kingdom of God, and if it tries to do so it becomes the greatest enemy of the kingdom of God. The political history of the Jewish people taught them to long for the coming of God's kingdom; but it could not itself bring that kingdom to them. For that the King Himself had to come; and when He did come, because He refused every kind of earthly kingship, the Jews utterly rejected Him.

(d) The clue to the Old Testament

The great themes of the Old Testament thus all point beyond themselves. They do not contain in themselves their own conclusion. They all end in a kind of self-contradiction. The work of the prophets (apart from Christ) ends in the barren self-righteousness of the Pharisees; the work of the priests (apart from Christ) ends in the priesthood of men like Annas and Caiaphas, no longer offering any hope of reconciliation for sinners and simply continuing an ancient ritual which had no power

[10] e.g. Isa. 11.1-12.
[11] John 6.15.
[12] e.g. John 18.11 and 36.
[13] Matt. 4.8-10.

to bring men to God; the quest for the kingdom of God (apart from Christ) ends in the futile revolts of the Jewish patriots after the death of Jesus, which brought down upon them the power of Rome and the final destruction of the Jewish State. Apart from Jesus, the true Prophet and King, the Old Testament ends in self-contradiction.

And yet the clue to the Old Testament is there, if only men could have seen it. What is the meaning of the strange story of this people—buffeted, battered, enslaved, crushed between great empires, dreaming of the kingdom of God and yet trampled under foot by every earthly kingdom? What is the meaning of this failure, this self-contradiction, this futility? Does it mean that there is no God? That is what most of the nations round about Israel thought, and mocked. 'Where is now thy God?' was the taunt which they constantly flung at Israel. Or does it mean that God is only waiting for the day when He will lay bare His arm, destroy all the other nations, and vindicate Israel in the eye of the world? That is what most of the Jews in the time of Jesus thought. But there was a voice in the Old Testament itself which had the answers to these questions; 'He was despised and rejected of men, a man of sorrows and acquainted with grief. . . . But he was wounded for our transgressions, he was bruised for our iniquities. . . . All we like sheep have gone astray; and the Lord hath laid on him the iniquity of us all.'[14] When the Jews of Jesus' time read those words, they could not understand them. We can even to-day study the commentaries they wrote, and can see that these words were incomprehensible. But Jesus knew that they contained the clue to the whole story of God's salvation— redemption through vicarious suffering. The whole story of Israel, and the story of individual servants of God such

[14] Isa. 52.13-53.12.

as Jeremiah and Isaiah, was pointing to this central truth —that God must save the world through the suffering, rejection, failure, defeat, shame of His Servant. The holy love of God can only make terms with the sin of men at the cost of suffering and death. That is the meaning of the strange self-contradiction of Israel's history. But that meaning could only be made plain when He Himself, both God and Man, came into the world as the true Prophet, Priest and King, to suffer and die for the sin of the world. Apart from Jesus the Old Testament is a self-contradiction. In the light of Jesus and His cross, we can understand that the whole story of God's people, from the call of Abraham to the coming of John the Baptist, was a preparation for just this work of salvation through Jesus Christ. To the study of that work of Christ we now turn.

VI

THE WORK OF THE SAVIOUR

(a) Introduction

G OD so loved the world, that he gave his only begotten son that whosoever believeth in him should not perish but have everlasting life.' In that sentence which every Christian knows and loves, the good news of salvation is briefly expressed. Let us examine it in detail as an introduction to our study.

1. The first thing we notice is that the author of our salvation is God. We have seen already that man is unable to extricate himself from the net of sin. Like an animal trapped in a clever snare, mankind trapped in the snare of sin struggles to free himself, but the more he struggles, the more the snare fastens its grip on him. His efforts to be free of sin are themselves infected by sin and drive him deeper into sin. Because sin is a corruption of the very centre of man's will, even when he wills to be free from sin he is driven deeper into sin.

This has become very clear in our study of the Old Testament. The more God's people strove to draw near to Him, the more deep was the gulf which separated them from Him. That is the tragedy of the Old Testament. And it reaches its climax in the Pharisees of the New Testament. These were the most zealous and energetic of the Jewish churchmen. They laboured unceasingly to bring the whole Jewish people under obedience to the Law of God. It was their aim to root out every trace of uncleanness in their lives and the life of their people. And yet it was these men who took the lead in the murder of Jesus. In that fact we see the nature of sin revealed. More than any other men, the Pharisees willed to escape from sin, but that very will drove them to the most terrible sin in the history of the world. Man can never by his own power or will extricate himself from the grip of sin; only God can extricate him. And God has done it. That is the good news which we preach.

2. Secondly we notice that this act of God sprang from His love for the world. We have seen that the whole world is in the power of sin, and is therefore in a state of enmity against God. And yet God loved the world and still loves it. That is the reason why He has put forth His power to save it. This is a fact which we must never forget. Sometimes Christians in trying to explain the cross of Christ have suggested that it was the love and self-sacrifice of Christ which turned away the wrath of God and so secured our salvation. This is a perversion of the truth. It is true that—as we have seen—the wrath of God is revealed against the sin of the world. The wrath of God is a reality. In order to understand the cross we must understand that. But the love which secured our salvation also comes from God. In Him there is both wrath and love. The wrath is the reverse side of His love. But God's wrath is not turned away by anything from outside of God. It was because God loved the world that He gave His Son to be its Saviour.

3. It is by giving His only begotten Son that God has saved the world. In order to understand this we have to speak briefly about the doctrine of the Holy Trinity. This is a mystery which is beyond the power of our human minds to understand fully. We must expect that the nature of God will be greater than our minds can grasp. But we have to try to understand what God has revealed

to us. He has revealed His nature to us as perfect love. In His being there is the complete fulness of love. This being so, we must say that God is personal but that He is not a person. For a single person cannot possess the fulness of love. Love in its fulness only exists where there is a giving and receiving of love, where love is mutual. If God were a single person, He could not know the perfection of love because there is no one who can give Him perfect love in return for His love. But what is revealed to us through Christ is a God in whom there is both giving and receiving of love, love in mutuality and in perfection. The Father loves the Son, and the Son loves the Father, and they are bound together in the same Holy Spirit. Of course this is more than our minds can grasp. There is one God, but He is not one Person; he is Father, Son and Holy Spirit. He is an ocean of love and joy beyond anything that we can conceive and beyond anything that could exist in one person. Out of that fulness the Son has come forth into the world to win our salvation. In so doing He has come under the power of sin and therefore under the sentence of suffering and death which is the wages of sin. But yet He remained and remains one with the Father in the unity of the Godhead. When He poured out His soul to death, He did not pour it out like water into sand; He poured it out into the hands of His Father. 'Father, into thy hands I commend my Spirit.' And the Father accepted the offering. Thus when God came forth to undertake the salvation of the world from sin, He did not abandon His Godhead. He remained and remains God, an ocean of love ever full, ever given and ever received, and therefore ever full of joy. How then did the Son come forth from the Father for the salvation of the world? He came 'in the likeness of sinful flesh';[1] He was 'made flesh';[2] He emptied Himself, taking

[1] Rom. 8.3.   [2] John 1.14.

the form of a servant, being found in fashion as a man.[3]
All these different phrases mean that He, being God, took
upon Himself our manhood—that manhood which has
come under the power of sin and death. The manhood
which He took was a complete manhood—body, mind
and soul. He was not a divine soul in a human body; He
was completely and perfectly a man. Nor was His manhood a temporary appearance. He took upon Him our
manhood for eternity. As man he rose from the dead and
ascended into heaven. This union of godhead and manhood in one person is certainly a mystery beyond our
comprehension. But the record of the apostles shows that
it is a fact. In the Gospel story we find that He is in every
respect a man like us. He is tempted by sin; He is wearied,
hungry, thirsty; He is disappointed and surprised by
unbelief; He longs for the companionship of His friends;
He is fully man. And yet at the same time He says things
and does things which only God can say and do. He takes
the Law of God from the Old Testament and says: 'Ye
have heard that it was said to them of old time thus . . .
But I say unto you . . .' Who but God can speak thus
—unless He be a blasphemer? Or consider such words as
these: 'He that loseth his life for my sake shall find it'[4]
or these: 'Whosoever shall be ashamed of me and of my
words in this adulterous and sinful generation, of him
shall the Son of man be ashamed when he cometh in the
glory of his Father with the holy angels.'[5] It is not necessary to give many examples; Jesus was a man who lived
among men in Palestine nineteen centuries ago; but He
also spoke and acted as God's own representative with full
powers to claim the obedience which man owes to God.
When the lord of the vineyard in Jesus' parable had sent
all His servants to claim His dues from the wicked culti-

[3] Phil. 2.7.   [4] Matt. 10.39.   [5] Mark 8.38.

vators, and when there was nothing more that He could do, He sent His own beloved son.[6] That is what God did for the world. He being 'God of God, Light of Light, Very God of Very God', came down from heaven and took upon Him our sinful manhood, was born of a virgin, lived a perfect human life, died, rose again, and ascended into heaven. Taking upon Himself our sinful nature, so that He became subject to the fierce temptations of sin as we are subject, He lived a life of sinless perfection in the midst of sin. Never for one moment did any evil come between Him and His Father. He remained at every instant 'in the bosom of the Father' in perfect intimacy with Him. Thus He met and overcame sin in our nature, from within the enemy's territory.

But when we have said this we have not yet reached the heart of the matter. The heart of the matter is His death. About that there can be no doubt. The New Testament makes this very clear. In the Gospels—where an account is given of His birth, life, teachings and miracles —the main attention is concentrated upon His sufferings and death and resurrection. In the Epistles this is even more clear. When St Paul gives a summary of the Christian message to the Corinthians,[7] it is entirely concerned with the death and resurrection. The rest of his teaching bears this out. His preaching is 'the word of the cross'.[8] And in the Epistles of Peter and John we find the same emphasis. In fact, as is well known, the cross has become the universal symbol of Christianity. The cross is the place where the decisive battle between Christ and sin took place, where the powers of Satan brought all their strength to the attack, and where they were defeated. It is the place where the wages of sin[9] were accepted on behalf of the whole human race.

[6] Mark 12.6.   [7] I Cor. 15.1-11.   [8] I Cor. 1.18-25.   [9] Rom. 6.23.

Of course the cross must not be isolated from the whole work of Christ. Without His incarnation there could be no cross and no salvation. Without His words and works we should not know who it was that died for us there. Without His resurrection the cross would not be known to us as victory but as defeat. Without His ascension to the Father and the gift of the Spirit, we who live at other times and places could have no share in Christ. All these things are parts of the one complete work of Christ for the salvation of the whole world. But the centre and focus of that work is the cross, and it is about the cross that we shall especially be speaking in the following chapters.

4. The verse which we are studying (John 3.16) goes on to say that the purpose of God's sending His Son was that 'those who believe on him should not perish but have everlasting life'. Everlasting life—that is the purpose. There is a way which goes to death. The whole world is on that way. It is going the way to death, destruction, emptiness, darkness. But God in His love does not will thus. He wills life for His creatures, He wills them to have it now. It is true that we cannot have the perfect fulness of life until God brings in the new heavens and the new earth which He has promised. The fulness is for all, and we cannot have it alone. We still have to take our place and bear our witness in the midst of this world which is under the power of death. Even our bodies must also die. But it is His will that, even now, we should be sharers in that eternal life. He gives this share through the Holy Spirit. By the gift of the Spirit we are able even now, while living in this world, to know that we are heirs of eternal life. It is given to us to have in us 'a well of water springing up unto life eternal'.[10]

5. Finally, our text tells us that it is by faith that we

[10] John 4.14.

are to take hold of this great blessing. What Christ has done once for all, in Palestine, nineteen centuries ago, can be made mine here to-day if I believe. Faith is the hand that grasps what Christ has done and makes it my own.

We have seen that the centre and heart of God's saving acts is the death of Jesus Christ on the cross. It is about that that we must now chiefly speak. It is important never to forget the whole saving work of which the cross forms only the centre. We must not isolate the cross and treat it in forgetfulness of what went before and what came after. Nevertheless the New Testament teaches us that when we seek the source of our salvation, it is primarily about the death of Christ that we have to speak.

As we try to do so, we must remember that, here too, we have a mystery which the mind of man can never fully grasp. Thousands of books have been written on the death of Christ. Many theories have been developed to explain how Christ's death saves us. And yet none of these theories really 'explains' it. All of them can only suggest, hint at, point to, the truth. The truth is that there is nothing else in all human experience which is equal to the cross, and therefore no general theory can explain it. But there are many helpful pictures and symbols given to us in the New Testament itself which—taken all together—help us to understand it. In what follows we shall first listen to what Jesus Himself taught about His death, and then look in turn at the main symbols which have been used to point to the meaning of the cross.

(b) The teaching of Jesus about His death

1. *His death is necessary.* Even in the earliest part of His ministry it appears that Jesus expected His death. He likens Himself and His disciples to a marriage-party,[11] and

[11] Mark 2.19-20.

says that the days are coming when the Bridegroom will be taken away. In many places the Messiah is likened to a bridegroom, and His coming to the joy of a marriage; but here He definitely warns them that the bridegroom will be taken away. Similarly in Mark 3.1-6 He makes it quite clear that he knows the Jews are planning His death. But it is after Peter's confession that He is the Christ, that Jesus begins very clearly to tell His disciples that He must die. 'The Son of man must suffer' is His repeated and emphatic word to them.[12] And in accordance with this we read that 'He steadfastly set his face to go to Jerusalem',[13] knowing that He was going to His death.

2. *His death is the will of the Father*. It is clear that Jesus did not merely accept His death as unavoidable on account of the forces which were ranged against Him; He accepted it as the will of His Heavenly Father. There is much evidence to show that He found the will of His Father expressed for Him in the prophecy of the Suffering Servant of the Lord,[14] which we have referred to in the last chapter. There are very frequent echoes of the language of this chapter in the Gospels. When He says to the twelve disciples 'How is it written of the Son of man that he should suffer many things and be set at naught'[15] He must have been referring to this chapter. And in Luke 22.37 He directly quotes it: 'I say unto you that this which is written must be fulfilled in me, And He was reckoned with transgressors.'

The matter becomes very clear in the prayer which Jesus made in the Garden of Gethsemane, 'Abba, Father, all things are possible unto thee, remove this cup from me; howbeit, not what I will, but what thou wilt'.[16]

[12] Mark 8.31; 9.31; 10.33-34. [15] Mark 9.12.
[13] Luke 9.51. [16] Mark 14.36.
[14] Isa. 53.

These words, and the whole of what happened in Gethsemane, make it very clear that Jesus accepted His death
not as something merely unavoidable, but as the means of
doing His Father's will. To suffer and die was not an
accident but the fulfilment of the vocation which God
had given Him.

3. *His death arises from His identification of Himself
with sinners.* At the outset of His ministry Jesus went to
be baptized by John in Jordan. This baptism was spoken
of as 'A baptism of repentance for the remission of sins'.[17]
Those who came to be baptized were men and women
who felt the burden of their sin and longed to be free of it.
It is very clear from Jesus' own words that He had no
personal burden of sin. He spoke always as one who had
unclouded fellowship with His Father without any of the
sense of sin which the greatest saints feel when they
approach God. And yet Jesus felt Himself so much one
with men, He loved them so much and identified Himself
with them so much that He gladly went with them to
share in the same baptism. It was then that He received
the definite assurance about His unique nature and
calling [18] and about the empowering of God's Spirit for
the task.[19] That was the beginning of His ministry as
Saviour of the world. And when He spoke about His death,
He spoke of it as the fulfilment, or accomplishment of His
baptism. 'I have a baptism to be baptized with, and how
am I straitened till it be accomplished.'[20] This identification of Himself with sinners reaches its climax in the
terrible cry from the cross: 'My God, my God, why hast
thou forsaken me?'[21] Here we see the sinless Son of God
crucified like a common criminal between two murderers,

[17] Mark 1.4.
[18] Mark 1.11.
[19] Mark 1.10.
[20] Luke 12.50.
[21] Mark 15.34.

so completely one with sinful men in their misery and shame, that He cries out—as it were—from the very pit of hell. He is 'made in all things like unto his brethren that he might be a merciful and faithful high priest in things pertaining to God, to make propitiation for the sins of the people'.[22]

4. *His death is God's judgment of the world.* One of the most memorable of Jesus' parables is the parable of the wicked husbandmen.[23] The basis of this parable is the famous parable of Isaiah about the vineyard.[24] It was a very familiar thought to all Jews that Israel was the vine-yard of the Lord, and that He had planted it in order to bring forth fruit. Jesus retells that story with new features. The Lord of the vineyard sends His servants one after another to receive the fruit, which is His due. One after another they are refused and humiliated. Obviously the reference is to the long line of great prophets. At last the Lord of the vineyard sends His 'Beloved Son' saying: 'They will reverence my Son'. And at once the wicked husbandmen take Him and kill Him and cast Him forth out of the vineyard. And the question follows: 'What will the Lord of the vineyard do?' It is obvious to all the hearers what this means. Jesus is the final Word of God to men; if they reject Him (as they are going to do) they will bring down upon themselves God's final judgment. And, to drive the point home, He adds another famous passage from the Old Testament: 'The stone which the builders rejected, the same was made the head of the corner; this was from the Lord and it is marvellous in our eyes'. Again the meaning is plain. He is Himself the head-stone. And in Luke's Gospel He adds: 'Every one that falleth on that stone shall be broken to pieces; but on whomsoever it shall fall it will scatter him as dust.'[25] The

[22] Heb. 2.17.   [23] Mark 12.1-9.   [24] Isa. 5.1-7.   [25] Luke 20.18.

C

crucifixion of Jesus is the decisive judgment of God upon the world.

5. *His death is a ransom.* In one of the most famous passages of the Gospels Jesus says: 'The Son of man came not to be ministered unto but to minister, and to give his life a ransom for many.'[26] In Psalm 49 (vv. 7-8) it is said: 'No one can by any means redeem his brother, nor give to God a ransom for him.' Jesus says that this is precisely what He has come to do. Men's souls are forfeit, ruined, lost. No man can redeem them. But Jesus has come to give His life as a ransom for them. In the original Greek it is very clear that He is giving His life not only for them but instead of them, that is, in their place. And the word translated 'ransom' is the same word which is translated in the Old Testament as propitiation. This word of Jesus does not tell us how His life is a ransom for many. But it tells us very clearly that He has come to give His life in place of, on behalf of, the lives of men which are forfeit.

6. *His death is a sacrifice.* We have seen that the word used in the previous saying for 'ransom' is a word which is used in the Old Testament in connection with sacrificial ideas. There is another saying in which the idea of sacrifice is made very clear. At the Last Supper, after Jesus had given bread to His disciples and said 'Take ye; this is my body', we read that He gave them the cup and said: 'This is my blood of the covenant, which is shed for many.'[27] What is meant by 'blood of the covenant'? There is little doubt that it refers to the giving of the covenant on Mount Sinai in the time of Moses. There we read that oxen were offered in sacrifice, part of the blood was sprinkled on the altar, and part of it was sprinkled on the people, and

---

[26] Mark 10.45.

[27] Mark 14.24; St Matthew's Gospel adds 'unto remission of sins', Matt. 26.28.

thereafter Moses and the elders of Israel were admitted to a vision of God and to eating and drinking in His presence.[28] Thus was the old covenant inaugurated: the blood of an animal was offered in sacrifice and by means of this God and the people were brought together. The meaning of Jesus' words seems to be that in the same way by the offering up of His life in sacrifice a new covenant between God and men is being inaugurated. Again, these words do not explain how a sacrifice such as this could remove sin and establish a new covenant between man and God. To understand that we have to understand the whole story of salvation. But they do show that Jesus regarded His death as a sacrifice which—like the ancient sacrifices—was intended to make atonement between God and man.

7. *His death is the means of life to the world.* In St John's Gospel there are a great many sayings in which Jesus reveals His belief that His death will be the means of new life for the world. This is the main subject of the long discourse in ch. 6 in which He speaks of Himself as the living bread come down from heaven. He says: 'The bread which I will give is my flesh for the life of the world.' In ch. 10 He speaks of Himself as the good shepherd who lays down His life for the sheep. He says He has come that they may have life and have it abundantly.[29] In ch. 12 he speaks of the corn of wheat which cannot bring forth new life except by falling into the ground and dying,[30] and of His being lifted up to draw all men to Himself.[31] These sayings are similar to His saying in Mark's Gospel: 'Whosoever would save his life shall lose it; and whosoever shall lose his life for my sake and the gospel's shall save it.'[32] We should here refer also

[28] Ex. 24.4-11.
[29] John 10.10-11.
[30] John 12.24-25.
[31] John 12.32.
[32] Mark 8.35.

to his saying about the temple which is given fully in
John's Gospel and also referred to in the others. [33] 'Destroy
this temple and in three days I will raise it up.' The
disciples did not understand this saying at the time, but
afterwards they understood. His death would bring into
being a new temple, a new dwelling place for God on
earth, namely the Church which is His body and wherein
men of every race can come together to find fellowship
with God.

8. *His death is not to be an isolated event, but others
are to follow it and share it.* According to St Mark, as
soon as Jesus began explicitly to speak of His death, He
also told His disciples that they must take up their crosses
and follow him.[34] As His death is the means of new life
to the world, so those who believe Him are to die with
Him and find new life through Him.[35] At the Last Supper
He calls upon His disciples to take and eat the bread which
is His broken body, and to drink the wine which is His
poured-out blood. In other words they are to be sharers
in His dying and new life. And in the Garden of Gethsemane He pleads with them to watch with Him, to be
sharers with Him in the agony of suffering for the world.
When they fall asleep in the midst of His agony, He is
deeply wounded and asks them: 'What, could ye not
watch with me one hour?'[36] His death is on behalf of all
men, instead of all men. He does something which man
cannot do for himself. But He wills that men should not
stand back and leave Him alone, but should share with
Him in His redemptive agony.

In the above eight paragraphs we have not looked at
all the sayings of Jesus which reveal His thought about His
death. There are many more which might be considered.

---

[33] John 2.19-22; cf. Mark 14.58 and 15.29.   [35] Mark 8.35.
[34] Mark 8.34.   [36] Matt. 26.40.

But these are sufficient to show how central was His death to the fulfilment of His mission. Yet, in spite of this teaching, we know that the disciples were not prepared for His death when it happened. In spite of all that had been said, it was so terrible that they were all broken by it and fled away. It was only after His resurrection that they could really understand its meaning. Thus for the fullest exposition of the meaning of His death we have to study the Epistles of Paul, John, Peter and other apostles. But when we study them, we find that their teaching is not different from the teaching which Jesus Himself had given before His crucifixion. Their teaching is based on their actual experience as men who had been forgiven and redeemed through the death of Christ. But it does not differ in essence from the teaching which the Redeemer had Himself given beforehand.

We have seen that the teaching of Jesus shows us very clearly what the cross does. It is the fulfilling of the Father's will; it is the culmination of Christ's self-identification with sinners; it is God's judgment upon the world; it is the means for man's redemption; it is a sacrifice; it is the way to new life for the world; and it is something in which believers are to be made participants. But it is inevitable that Christians should ask how the cross accomplishes these things. When we begin to ask this question we soon get into great difficulties. In the nineteen centuries of Christian theology there have been many theories about the cross. All have some truth in them, but none of them alone contains the whole truth. The cross in a greater mystery than can be contained in a single theory. And yet we must use our minds to try to understand how Christ is our Redeemer and the Author of new life for us. In the remainder of this chapter we shall try to answer this question following several lines of thought, and looking at the teaching of the later parts of the New Testament.

(c) *The death of Jesus a revelation of God's love*

Everyone who has studied the Gospels at all will agree about this, that Jesus loved men, women and children. He made Himself one with them, even with those who were most degraded and sinful. He spent Himself in their service, pouring out His soul in healing power upon the sick, the cripples, the lepers, and all who were in need. In His dealings with individuals, especially with His own disciples, He showed a tender love and understanding for each one. And not only so, he brought to them the forgiveness of their sins. To the paralytic boy who was let down at His feet through the roof, to the sinful woman who came into Simon's house during a feast, and to many others He said 'Thy sins are forgiven thee'. He brought, that is to say, not only healing and help to body and mind; He also brought to the souls of men release from the grip of sin. He made them free as children of God— free as He Himself was free.

It was at this point that Jesus came into serious conflict with the Jewish authorities. 'Why doth this man thus speak?' they said. 'He blasphemeth: who can forgive sins but one, even God?'[37] If Jesus is only a man, then the Jews were right. Only God can forgive sins. If a man has done wrong to me, only I can forgive him. It is useless for someone else to say 'I forgive you'. The person against whom the sin was done is the person who must forgive it. But if Jesus was truly God incarnate—as He believed and His disciples believed—then His word of forgiveness was not blasphemy. He was actually the means by which God was bringing His forgiveness to sinful men. In His words,

[37] Mark 2.7.

in His deeds of healing, and in His whole life, He was bringing the love of God to sinful man. That is what He Himself believed about His own work. Everything He did was simply the doing of His Father's will.[38] He is the beloved Son of the Father come down to bring the Father's love to the world. He is the good shepherd seeking the lost sheep. As St Paul says: 'God was in Christ reconciling the world unto himself'.[39]

And no one will doubt that in this respect His death was the continuation and climax of His life. As St John says, 'Having loved his own, he loved them to the uttermost'.[40] The pouring out of His soul in His daily ministry culminated in the pouring out of His soul unto death on the cross. His identification of Himself with sinful men in life culminated in His dying the death of a sinner between two sinners on Calvary. His death, like His life, was a manifestation of love: 'No man taketh my life from me, I lay it down of myself.'[41] But this act is not simply His act; it is the fulfilling of the will of God through Him: 'This commandment received I from my Father.' As St Paul says: 'God commendeth his own love for us in that, while we were yet sinners, Christ died for us.'[42] The death of Christ is the revelation of the love of God.

It is important for us to note that the love of God can only be revealed by an act. Words alone cannot reveal love. Even if God were to write the words 'God is Love' in letters of fire in the clouds, it would not tell us anything. Love must be expressed in deeds. When we see a man's deeds we know whether we can believe his words. It is easy to talk about the love of God. We cannot know

[38] See John 5.19; this whole chapter is an explanation of the meaning of the healing works of Jesus.
[39] II Cor. 5.19.   [41] John 10.18.
[40] John 13.1.   [42] Rom. 5.8.

the love of God except by seeing what He has done for the salvation of the world. What He has done is to give His beloved Son to the death of the cross.

But when all this has been said, there are still two serious difficulties which have to be considered. The first is this: love must be shown not only in deeds, but in deeds which are actually directed to the need of the other person. If I am drowning in a well and another man jumps into the well and rescues me, while he himself is drowned in the effort, then there can be no doubt about that man's love. He has given his life for me. But if I am attacked by a tiger I need a different kind of help. My friend may jump into the well and drown himself, but that will not rescue me from the tiger. In that case, even though my friend gave up his life, I cannot say that he loved me or saved me. Christ gave up His life on the cross, but how does that save me? How does it rescue me from my sin? Unless we can show that there is some connection between Christ's death and my sin I cannot believe that Christ's death is a proof of love for me, or that it has saved me from sin. Clearly it is not enough simply to say that the cross is a revelation of God's love, unless we can answer these questions.

The second difficulty is this: how is it possible for sins to be forgiven? This question needs to be very carefully thought about. Let us consider a simple example with which we are familiar. An official in charge of a big Government office, such as a Collector,[43] has to be responsible for the good discipline of that office. When faults are discovered—corruption, laziness, inefficiency, etc.—he has to take some action. Some officers are very

[43] 'In India, the chief administrative officer of a district, whose special duy is the collection of Revenue' (*Shorter Oxford English Dictionary*).

strict. Others are slack and easily allow faults to be excused. We know well in our own experience that when this happens, the whole department becomes rotten, so that it becomes almost impossible even for a very honest man to remain honest and work there. Unless there is discipline, punishment, if necessary dismissal of bad workers, the department is bound to become rotten. It is true that even a very strict officer will sometimes forgive faults—indeed he must do so. But always this forgiveness is against a background of authority and discipline. The man who is forgiven knows that if he commits the same fault again he will be severely punished, and that if he goes on doing it, he will be dismissed. Supposing a District Collector issued a notice which said: 'All faults committed by the staff of this office, past, present and future, are hereby forgiven' we know that the result would be chaos and disaster. How, then, could God give such a notice to the world? It is not enough to say of the cross: 'God in His love and pity has forgiven all the sins of the world', unless we understand how that forgiveness is given. If God forgave sins without at the same time judging and punishing them, the world would be a chaos and there would no longer be any things called 'right' and 'wrong'.

We shall try to consider this objection further in the next section when we speak of the cross as judgment, and the other objection in the following section on 'The cross as ransom'.

(d) *The death of Jesus as a judgment*

We have seen that in the teaching of Jesus Himself, the cross is seen as God's judgment upon the sin of His people. This thought is also repeated many times in the Epistles of St Paul. God, he says, 'sending his own Son in the like-

ness of sinful flesh and as an offering for sin, condemned
sin in the flesh'.[44] The cross was the revelation of God's
righteousness[45] and therefore necessarily constitutes a
judgment of the sin of the world. We can explain this in
three ways.

1. In the first place it is very obvious that the cross
exposes, shows up, the rule of sin in the world. As He
Himself said,[46] His coming was like the coming of a great
light which causes men to oppose it because it shows up
their evil works. Of course all men at all times admit that
there is sin in the world, that things are done which
ought not to be done, that men are not what they ought
to be. But most men usually believe that the sin is in
others: they make a distinction between the good men,
moralists, pious people, who are seeking to do good (even
with occasional lapses) and the rest who do not care. But
what was revealed in the light of Christ is something new
and terrible. It is that *all* men are traitors against the light.
In the time of Jesus the most zealous, hardworking and
popular religious leaders were the Pharisees; they were
trying to apply the ancient law of Moses to the conditions
of the day, to insist on the strict keeping of the whole
Law of God, and to bring the blessings of religion to all
people through the synagogue services. Yet when the Son
of man came these men were the leaders in the plan to
kill Him. In the time of Jesus the most just, stable, and
honest political system was the Roman empire. It was
trying to keep the whole known world together in a single
peace, with just laws, good roads, and security against
invasion. Yet it was the Roman governor who (in order to
avoid a riot) handed Jesus over to execution. In the time
of Jesus the political leaders were the Sadducees and the
high priestly party. They were trying to preserve the

[44] Rom. 8.3.   [45] Rom. 3.21-26.   [46] John 3.19.

Jewish religion, the Temple services, and the sacrifices in the midst of the alien Roman rule. It was the anointed high priest who condemned Jesus as blasphemer. The ordinary common people, who had at first received Jesus joyfully as their leader, when they had to make a choice between Him and a popular revolutionary leader who had been arrested for sedition, chose Barabbas and rejected Jesus. And finally, even of Jesus' own disciples one betrayed Him, one denied, the rest forsook Him and fled. The death of Jesus was not the work of a few scoundrels whom all the world would afterwards condemn; it was the action of the whole people. Although at first many had joyfully followed the light, at the end they could not endure it. In that light it was not possible for anyone to call himself righteous. And in the end, all men conspired together to blot it out. Here and here only we understand the true position of the human race before God. We see that the human race, which has so much pride in its own learning, its own righteousness, its own piety, is in truth a rebel gang, at enmity with God. It is like the wicked husbandmen who behave as if God's vineyard were their own and kill the heir when He comes for the fruits. When we understand this, we realize that we can deserve nothing except death. We realize the awfulness of sin. We hear in our ears the terrible words of Jesus: 'What therefore will the lord of the vineyard do? he will come and destroy the husbandmen and give the vineyard to others'. We know that God's just judgment has been pronounced on us.

2. In the second place, we can see God's judgment pronounced upon human sin in the cross, in the way that Jesus met and overcame evil. We have seen that the coming of Jesus was like the coming of a light which showed up the evil that before was hidden. But it was not

only that. Jesus actively went out to meet evil and to overcome it with good. There are no words so terrible in all
the Bible as the words with which Jesus denounced the
evil that He found in men who were supposed to be good.
He exposed and denounced the hidden pride and loveless-
ness of the Pharisees. He gave terrible warnings to those
who put stumbling blocks in the way of those who are
children in faith.[47] He publicly attacked the commercial
interests which had made the Temple into a den of thieves.
He deliberately broke the Jewish laws when they were
being used to shut men and women out of life. In the
face of every kind of hypocrisy and lying He steadfastly
witnessed to the truth. And when all this led to opposition
and finally to the plot to kill Him, He neither retreated
nor fought back, but gave Himself up for the sake of the
truth. Thus as it were He flung His whole self, soul and
body, in the path of evil—exposing it, taking its assault
upon Himself, and destroying its power. The final culmination of all this is His cross. There not merely as a
passive victim, but as an active warrior beating down the
powers of evil, He condemned sin publicly before the eyes
of men. Evil wins most of its victories by deceit, by pre-
tending to be good, by confusing and blinding men's eyes
so that they cannot distinguish good from evil. Jesus tore
all this subterfuge aside, exposed evil in its true nature,
endured the whole assault of its power, and remained
steadfast in love and purity to the end. Therefore He condemned it.

3. There is still something more that has to be said
about the cross as a judgment upon sin. The New Testament contains some very strong expressions of the truth
that God in some sense condemned the sin of the world
in Jesus. 'Him who knew no sin he made to be sin on our

[47] Matt. 18.6.

behalf, that we might become the righteousness of God in him.'[48] 'Christ Jesus redeemed us from the curse of the law, having become a curse for us.'[49] And these verses echo the mysterious words in Isaiah 53: 'The Lord hath laid on him the iniquity of us all.' How are we to understand these words? It is easy to twist them so that they make it appear that God is a cruel and immoral ruler. How can we believe that God punished Jesus for the sins of others? Would not that mean that God was wicked and unjust? And would it not mean that wicked men could sin believing that they will not be punished? We have to think carefully about this if we are to understand it rightly.

God is holy and He has made us that we may live in holy love with Him. Therefore, although He has given us freedom and responsibility to turn away from Him or to turn to Him, He does not allow sin to go unchecked. He is not like a slack official who allows things to slide. He resists sin with wrath, punishes it, brings it to ruin. He so orders the universe that sin brings suffering, disaster, and death. But (and this is very important) He does not so order it that each man's suffering is proportionate to his sin. Very clearly we suffer for one another's sin. If this were not so there could be no love in the world. Love leads us to bear one another's burdens and share one another's troubles. If we could not do that, there could be no love. Because God is holy love, He has so ordered the universe not only so that sin brings suffering, but also so that the suffering is shared.

But now we must notice another thing. When a sinful man suffers because of his sins, he usually does not understand it as God's righteous judgment. He thinks it is bad luck, or fate, or someone else's fault. He curses it and

[48] II Cor. 5.21.   [49] Gal. 3.13.

hates it. When he begins to understand his suffering as God's righteous judgment, he has already begun to repent. On the other hand a good man or woman will understand suffering, even if it is caused by another, as God's righteous judgment, because he will understand how terrible a thing sin is. The more a man is filled with the love of God the more he will be willing to take the sorrows and sufferings of others upon himself, and the more he will be willing to accept them as God's just judgment upon the sin of the world. Only the perfectly good man would be able to feel perfectly the judgment of God upon human sin, and to take upon himself all the burden of that suffering. The sinner cannot begin to do it until he has begun to turn from his sin. We see this illustrated in the two thieves who were crucified with Jesus.[50] One was impenitent and could not do anything but mock at Christ and cry out to be set free. The other had begun to repent and could acknowledge that his sufferings were just.

Only the perfectly good man could perfectly feel the judgment of God upon sin, and take upon himself all the burden of it. There was no man good enough, so God gave His only Son to take our manhood and do just that. He who alone was sinless alone could take upon Himself the whole burden of our sin and suffer for it, accepting that suffering as God's just judgment upon sin. It is a paradox, but it is true, that only the sinless could offer true repentance. And it is through His offering that we can begin to repent. We only understand God's judgment upon sin when we see it in the sinless One. The penitent thief began to understand that God's judgment was just, and began to repent of his sin, when he saw the righteous One suffering alongside of him. 'We receive the due reward of our deeds, but this man hath done nothing amiss.'[51]

[50] Luke 23.39-43.   [51] Luke 23.41.

Thus when we say that Jesus bore the punishment of our sins, that He became a curse for us, that 'God made Him to be sin for us' we are not saying something which contradicts the rest of human experience. Our salvation through Christ is possible because God has so made us that we should be able to bear one another's burdens. In an earlier chapter we saw that sin is like a snare which man cannot escape from, because his efforts to escape tighten its grip upon him. He cannot be forgiven until he truly repents, but repentance is precisely what is impossible to him. Repentance means having a new mind, forsaking my own mind which is at enmity with God, and having a new mind. That new mind cannot come from myself. But when we see what happened on Calvary, where the sin of the world was exposed in all its terrible wickedness, where Jesus flung Himself against it, and where in humble obedience He—the sinless One—accepted in His own soul the just judgment of God upon human sin, there repentance is made possible to us, as to the dying thief. There we understand that forgiveness does not mean being freed from punishment. (That is what the impenitent thief thought.)[52] We understand that the ordinance of God by which sin leads to suffering and death is just; we accept that ordinance as He accepted it. But when we see Him there, the sinless One for love of men taking their sin upon Himself, dying a sinner's death along with sinners, making no difference between Himself and them but being numbered among the transgressors, then there is born in us a new mind—the new mind which made the other thief say: 'Lord remember me when thou comest in thy kingdom'. In the first place there is a real repentance; we have to accept the judgment which Jesus has accepted for us. In the second place there is faith; He

[52] Luke 23.39.

is beside us, giving Himself for us: therefore in life or in death we can trust Him. Thus the bond between us and God which sin had broken is restored here—not by our reaching up to God by the strength of our own repentance, but by His coming down beside us to die a sinner's death. This is true forgiveness—not the remitting of a penalty, but the restoring of the bond of love which had been broken. The penalty still has to be borne. But He is bearing it for us, and with us, and now inviting us freely to bear it with Him for others.

It has been truly said that 'the living conscience can only accept forgiveness along with judgment'. If there is no judgment then there was no sin: if there was no sin there is no need of forgiveness. If God simply forgave without also judging, He would be like a slack and corrupt officer. The world would quickly go to ruin. Forgiveness means that I first accept God's judgment upon me as a sinner, and only in the midst of that condemnation I find that God yet holds me to Himself as a beloved son.

(e) The death of Jesus as ransom

We read in the Old Testament much about the redemption of those who had been sold into slavery, and about the duty of a man to redeem his poor kinsman who has been sold into slavery because of poverty.[53] This common social custom provided the Hebrew prophet with language to describe the saving work of God. God is described as the Redeemer of Israel, who has rescued them out of slavery in Egypt, and who will again rescue them from Babylon. This idea is repeatedly expressed in Isaiah (e.g. 41.14; 43.1; 44.6; 47.4; 60.16, etc.). In these passages not much is usually said about the price paid for ransom, but in Isaiah 43.3 it is said that God has given three

[53] e.g. Lev. 25.47-55.

countries in Egypt as a ransom price for Israel to the Persian king.

In the New Testament this idea of ransom is used very frequently when speaking of what Jesus has done for us, but here the ransom-price is very much emphasized. The ransom-price is nothing less than Jesus Himself, His own life-blood. We have already noticed His own saying: 'The Son of Man came . . . to give his life as ransom for many.'[54] Similarly St Peter says (I Peter 1.18): 'Ye were redeemed, not with corruptible things, with silver or gold . . . but with precious blood as of a lamb without blemish and without spot, even the blood of Jesus'. St Paul, likewise, speaks of our redemption that is in Christ Jesus, whom God set to be a propitiation through faith by His blood,[55] and in many other places also he speaks of our being redeemed by the death of Christ.

In one respect we can all immediately see that this idea of ransom, or redemption, is a very suitable one to describe what Christ has done, for it is clear that the state from which He has come to rescue us is a state of slavery. We have already seen in the earlier part of this book that sin has brought the human race into a state of bondage from which man cannot extricate himself. Man is indeed like one who has been sold into slavery. His life is forfeit. His will is no longer free. He is under a curse.[56] Although he knows what is good, he is unable to do what is good.[57] He is a prisoner unable to set himself free. And Christ has done what man could not do for himself; He has set him free at the cost of His own blood.

Yet the metaphor of ransom cannot be pressed too far. In the early Church the question was asked: 'If Christ redeemed us by paying the ransom-price of His own blood, to whom was the price paid? Was it to God or to the

[54] Mark 10.45.   [55] Rom. 3.24 ff.   [56] Gal. 3.13.   [57] Rom. 7.7-24.

devil?' If we say 'to God', then we set Jesus against the Father, as though the Father were a hard-hearted merchant who would only release the slave for payment. But in truth we know that it was from God Himself that the ransom price came. 'God so loved the world that he gave his only begotten Son.' Recognizing this, some ancient writers tried to show that the price was paid to Satan. Some even taught that Jesus was like the bait with which the fisherman baits his hook. Satan was deceived by the humanity of Jesus and swallowed Him up, but the divine nature in Him was like the hook which caught Satan unawares. Such theories are obviously misguided. Jesus on the cross did not deliver Himself to Satan. On the contrary, He said: 'Father, into thy hands I commend my spirit.' We cannot press the metaphor of ransom to the point of saying that the price was paid to God or to Satan.

And yet a price had to be paid. We have seen already that Jesus regarded His death as necessary for the salvation of the world. At no less price could man be saved out of the bondage of sin. But how did Christ's death redeem us from this bondage? How is His death related to my sin? We cannot fully answer that question until we come to speak of our union with Christ through faith. But here we can say this: Christ by His death has put Himself completely in our place. The final issue of our sin is death. Death is, as St Paul says, the wages of sin. It is the final harvest that sin yields. All our experience of bondage, our inability to do that which we know to be right, finds its culmination in the fact of death. Even though we may overcome every other enemy, death finally overcomes us. That is the outward sign, so to speak, of the fact that we have forfeited our inheritance of life. Although created in the image of the eternal God, we have become subject to death on account of sin. What Jesus has done is to put Himself completely under this same bondage, with us and for us and as one of us. He has not only taken upon Himself our sin-polluted nature, and lived a human life under the conditions created by sin; He has also gone with us to the last limit and died that death which is the wages of sin, died and risen again. By that fact our whole situation is changed. For, as He has made Himself one with men in their death, so He has made it possible for men to be made one with Him in His life. How that is so we shall see when we come to speak of our union with Christ. Here what is clear is that no union of our sinful selves with the Holy One would be possible if He had not first come down to make Himself one with us in our bondage to death. By giving Himself to bondage and death, coming under the curse of sin, submitting meekly to all that sentence of pain and shame and death which the holiness of God must pronounce upon the sin of man, He made it possible for us to be delivered from that sentence and that bondage. In very truth He has redeemed us by His blood.

(f) The death of Jesus as sacrifice

In the last section, when speaking of the death of Christ as a ransom, we quoted the words of Peter: 'Ye were redeemed not with corruptible things, with silver or gold . . . but with precious blood as of a lamb without blemish and without spot, even the blood of Christ.'[58] It is clear that in this passage the writer is thinking of the death of Jesus not only as a ransom but also as a sacrifice. He is thinking of the lambs which were sacrificed daily in the Temple at Jerusalem according to the Jewish law. Similarly when Jesus Himself spoke of His purpose to 'give his life a ransom for many', there is an echo in His words

[58] I Peter 1.18-19.

of the words of Isaiah 53.10-12 where it is said that the
Servant of the Lord will be made a guilt-offering, that is a
sacrifice. We have also seen already that the words used
by our Lord at the Last Supper show that He regards His
death as a sacrifice. In His baptism, when He identified
Himself once for all with sinners, He saw the Spirit
descending upon Him as a dove—the poor man's sacrifice.[59] And, according to St John's Gospel, He was
recognized even in His life as 'the Lamb of God that taketh
away the sin of the world', that is, the lamb of sacrifice.
This idea of sacrifice is clearly one of the clues which will
help us to understand the death of Jesus. But if we are to
follow it, we must ask not What does the word sacrifice
mean to us here to-day, but What did the word mean for
Jews in the time of Jesus? And to answer that question
we must look at the Old Testament.

It is not possible here to speak at length about the sacrificial laws of the Old Testament as they are contained in
Leviticus and other books. It is sufficient to note two fundamental principles: 1. The sacrifices are ordained by
God. They are part of the covenant which He makes with
His people. The system of sacrifice is not something
invented by the people; it is provided by God. This is a
point of very great importance. Man does not and cannot
propitiate God. In the Old Testament the verb meaning
'to make propitiation' occurs very frequently. But it never
occurs with 'God' as its object. In the nations round about
Israel it was a very common idea that man could propitiate God by sacrifice and gifts; but this idea was absolutely excluded from the Old Testament. The whole
system of sacrifice is provided by God, and given to man
as the way by which he should approach Him. It is a part
of God's gracious covenant. It springs out of the love of

[59] Mark 1.9-11.

God, not out of men's need to propitiate God's wrath.
2. But at the same time, the sacrifices which the Law pre-
scribes are to be offered by men to God, and their purpose
is 'to make atonement' or 'make propitiation'. This is the
condition upon which sinful man can approach the Holy
One. Man. who is in a state of rebellion against God,
cannot walk into the house of God and sit down to meat
as though he were walking into the house of a friend.
That would be an impossibility. A direct meeting between
man and God could only mean that man was utterly destroyed. Nor will God act as though there were no sin
between them; there is no 'make-believe' about His dealing
with us. He is the Holy One, and He will not behave as
though He were otherwise. Something has to be done
about the sin of man before he can hold fellowship with
God. What can be done? Man cannot make any offering
which would be adequate to atone for his sin. Nor can God
merely wipe away man's sin as if it were a dirty mark
on the face, for the sin is a perversion of man's will, and
only when man's will is converted is his sin taken away.
What, then, is the way for sinful man to come near to
God?

The answer of the Old Testament is that God has provided a way—the way of sacrifice. When man comes into
God's presence, he must offer a life to God. It is important
to understand that what is offered in sacrifices is not a
dead carcase, but the blood, which means the life of the
animal. Man's life as a sinner is forfeit; he is doomed to
die. But God allows him to bring a life in his stead and to
offer that as he comes to worship. Thus the way to God
is marked by signs which are a perpetual reminder of the
fact that between man and God there lies the gulf of sin,
and that the wages of sin is death. The way is provided by
God; but man must offer to God the sacrifices which He

has prescribed in order to have fellowship with Him.

And yet it remains true that all these things are only signs, without power to effect what they signify. The blood of goats and bulls cannot cleanse the conscience. That is a fact of which the prophets were constantly reminding Israel. What God wants is not the blood of animals, but the life of man—his heart and soul and body, his love and obedience. And yet that is what man, caught in the snare of sin, cannot give. Man must give it, and yet man cannot? Can God give it for him, and if so, how can that gift help man?

The answer of the New Testament is that God has Himself provided the sacrifice, as He did for Abraham on Mount Moriah.[60] The sacrifice is Jesus, who is both God and Man. In Him alone a perfect offering of love and obedience has been made to the Father, and therefore He is the Lamb of God that taketh away the sins of the world. This teaching is most fully worked out in the Epistle to Hebrews. The author shows that the sacrifices of the Jewish Law are powerless to reconcile man with God[61] and that what God wills is not sacrifice but obedience.[62] Then He shows that it is in the perfect obedience of Jesus that the one perfect sacrifice for sin has been made.[63] And he goes on to say to his fellow-believers that they have 'boldness to enter into the holy place by the blood of Jesus, by the way which he dedicated for us, a new and living way through the veil, that is to say his flesh'.[64] In the ancient sacrifices, the worshippers drew near to God through the sacrifice—offering up their lives symbolically in the life of the slain animal. Now men can draw near to God through Christ who is the one perfect sacrifice. But

[60] Gen. 22.1-13.
[61] Heb. 10.1-4.
[62] Heb. 10.5-9.
[63] Heb. 10.10-18
[64] Heb. 10.19-20

now they do not offer themselves merely in a symbol; they are truly made one with Him, and they offer themselves up to the Father in Him and through Him. Because of our sin we cannot of ourselves offer an acceptable sacrifice to God; He alone can do so. But because He has done so in the flesh, that is as a man, and because He unites us to Himself in His human nature; we can offer ourselves in and through Him. That is part of the meaning of the serevice of Holy Communion, and that is why in the Church of South India Liturgy we use these words from Hebrews at the beginning of the Service of Breaking Bread: 'O God who through thy son Jesus Christ hast opened for us a new and living way unto thy throne of Grace.'

The death of Jesus thus provides in reality what the sacrifices of the Old Testament provided only in symbol. He is the mercy seat, the place where sinful men may meet with the Holy God. In His death He has made the perfect offering of human life to God, the perfect submission to God's just punishment of sin and the perfect offering of sorrow for sin. This is what man cannot do, because of his sin. But because Christ has done it, there is a place where God's love can meet with men without lessening the majesty of His holiness. There is a place where both God's judgment and God's mercy can be known together. And sinful man, acknowledging both the judgment and the mercy, is brought to the same self-offering. In and through Christ he is able to do what he could not do apart from Christ—offer himself up, body and soul, to the Father. Thus Jesus is the Lamb of God who—not just in symbol but in reality—takes away the sin of the world; for the root of sin is man's distrust of God. The death of Christ makes it possible for that distrust to be replaced by humble and obedient faith.

(g) The death of Jesus as victory

There are several passages, especially in the Fourth Gospel, which show that Jesus looked upon His death as the climax of a great struggle with the powers of evil. Early in His ministry He spoke of His own ministry in these terms. When challenged on His healing miracles he said: 'If I by the finger of God cast out (demons) then is the kingdom of God upon you', and likened Himself to a successful robber who is strong enough to overpower the lord of this world and rob him of his goods.[65] In the Fourth Gospel he speaks of His death as the casting out of the prince of this world.[66] In St Paul's Epistle to the Colossians the cross is depicted as a mighty victory in which Christ has openly triumphed over the powers of evil, and put them to open defeat,[67] and in the first Epistle of John it is said that the purpose of Christ's coming is to 'destroy the works of the devil', words which mind us of His own words, 'I beheld Satan falling as lightning from heaven.'[68] When we remember that the beginning of His ministry was marked by the tremendous struggle in the wilderness, when for forty days He wrestled with temptation, we can understand how this language of battle and victory came to have such a place in His own words and in those of His disciples.

If we take the temptations in the wilderness as our clue, we shall best understand the victory of the cross. In those temptations we see how He was tempted to use other methods than God's methods in order to serve God's kingdom. He was tempted to build success on men's hunger, on their love of marvel, or on their need for political order. When He rejected all these, He went out to face

[65] Luke 11.20-22.
[66] John 12.31.
[67] Col. 2.15.
[68] I John 3.8; Luke 10.18.

the world completely unarmed as far as all ordinary earthly armament is concerned, armed only with the love of God. That decision took Him to the cross. It meant that He had to let all the hate and envy and fear of men come home on to his own heart. We know that He was tempted to forsake that way. When Peter in a friendly way tried to tell Him that He would escape the cross, He recognized the voice of the Tempter and turned and said: 'Get thee behind me, Satan'.[69] When He 'steadfastly set his face to go up to Jerusalem',[70] we can be sure that He was facing a fierce inward conflict. This conflict came to its climax in the Garden of Gethsemane. It is quite impossible for us to understand fully what He endured during those hours of prayer in the Garden. It was a conflict so terrible that even the Author and Finisher of our Faith was brought to His knees in an agony of bloody sweat. All the powers of hell were let loose upon Him to shake Him from His purpose. All the wickedness and hatred and treachery that the devil and his angels have let loose in the world gathered together around His head. But nothing was able to shake Him from His simple determination to do His Father's will, even if it meant apparently total defeat, the scattering of His beloved disciples and His own shameful death —the death that every Jew counted accursed. When He had endured the agony of dereliction on the cross, when He had endured not only agony and shame, but even the sense that God Himself had deserted Him, at the end He could cry 'It is finished'. Then, knowing that the victory was won He gave back His Spirit to His Father. When we were speaking about corporate guilt and temptation we were reminded of the fact that behind all human evil there is a superhuman organization of evil, a strategy of wickedness beyond any human contriving. There is the usurped

[69] Mark 8.33.   [70] Luke 9.51.

power of Satan. On account of sin man has fallen under
the power of Satan and is unable to free himself. But by
His obedience unto death Christ has decisively broken that
evil dominion. Satan's power on that day received a defeat
from which it can never recover. Henceforth even though
the remnants of that power may seem very impressive,
those who are in Christ know that it is broken. The Name
of Jesus on the lips and in the heart of a believer is enough
to banish the power of Satan. We cannot understand fully
how that victory was won, but it is in the power of that
victory that the Church lives. When Jesus had risen from
the dead and reunited His scattered disciples, He told
them: 'All power is given unto me in heaven and in
earth'. That is the basis of the Christian mission to the
world. It is in the power of His completed victory that
His people have gone out into all the world to beat down
the kingdom of Satan and proclaim the kingdom of God.

(h) *The resurrection and ascension of Jesus*

All that has been said so far about the death of Jesus,
can be said only in the light of the resurrection. If the
body of Jesus had remained in the tomb to moulder like
any other human corpse, the disciples would never have
returned to Jerusalem, there would have been no Pentecost, no Christian preaching, and no Christian faith. Jesus
would have been only another martyr. Because of the
resurrection we know that Jesus is more. Because He is
the Holy One, therefore 'It was not possible for him to be
holden of death'.[71] By the evidence of the empty tomb,
and still more by the evidence of His own risen presence
with them, the disciples knew that His death was not
defeat but victory. During the forty days that He spent
with them He interpreted to them the meaning of His

[71] Acts 2.24.

death.[72] They learned that He was alive and victorious, that all power had been given to Him, and that they were to go out into all the world to proclaim His victory.

This period of forty days was followed by the event which we call the ascension, when His visible presence was withdrawn from them. Hitherto they had known Him —even after His resurrection—through the five senses, as we may know any other man. As long as this was so, it is plain that He could only be known to a small circle of intimate friends of that place and time. In order that He might fulfil His vocation to be the Saviour of the whole world, it was necessary that He should be withdrawn from the reach of the five senses and be known through the Spirit. Therefore when He had fully made known to the disciples what they needed to know about the meaning and purpose of His life and death He withdrew from their touch and sight, promising them the gift of the Spirit to empower them to be His witnesses to the end of the world and to the farthest parts of the earth.

Thus we may say that the Saviour's earthly work was completed. And yet in another sense we must say that salvation is not complete until it is complete in the experience of the men whom He came to save. We cannot, indeed, understand the work of Christ until we see how what He has done for us becomes our possession. To answer that question is the business of the next chapter.

[72] Luke 24.25-27.

VII

HOW SALVATION BECOMES OURS

(a) The Church

IN the preceding chapter we have spoken of what Jesus
has done on behalf of men. He has done for them
what they cannot do for themselves—overcome the
powers of evil, offered up the perfect sacrifice for the sin
of the world, given the only ransom-price by which the
souls of men could be redeemed. He has made Himself
completely one with sinful men, offered on their behalf
the penitence and obedience which they cannot offer,
endured for men's sake God's condemnation of the sin of
men. But the question still has to be answered: Where
do I come into this? What is the connection between this
work of Christ in Palestine two thousand years ago, and
my sin to-day? It is to that question that we have now
to address ourselves.

When we look at the record, what strikes us is that the
story of Jesus has reached us through a group of men and
women who were so closely bound to Him that their life
could almost be spoken of as an extension of His life.
They speak of themselves as being 'in Christ'—a phrase
used by Paul scores of times—of being 'the Body of Christ'
of being 'partakers of Christ'.[1] They can speak of 'Christ
who is our life',[2] of 'Christ in you, the hope of glory'.[3]
One of them can say: 'I live, yet no longer I but Christ

[1] Heb. 3.14   [2] Col. 3.4.   [3] Col. 1.27.

lives in me'.[4] In fact they speak as though the fellowship to which they belonged was verily an extension of Christ's own person, so that they are not separate from Him, but so much part of Him that He is in them and they in Him.

This being so, when they speak of the death of Christ and of His resurrection, they do not speak of them as things which are—so to speak—external to themselves, remote events of which they have merely heard a report. They speak of them as events in which they themselves have shared. 'I have been crucified with Christ.'[5] 'All ye who were baptized were baptized into his death.'[6] 'Ye are risen with Christ.'[7] God 'has raised us up with Christ and made us to sit with him in the heavenly places'.[8] However we are to explain his language, it certainly means this: that those who wrote it felt themselves to be so bound up with Him that what He had done had become their own, so that when they came before God they came, so to say, in the person of Christ—in His Name and as part of Him. They are His and He is theirs. Their righteousness is not their own, but His[9] and so also is their wisdom and their holiness.[10] Everything that they have is His; their very existence is 'in Christ'.

Thus we can give the first and simplest answer to the question: 'How does what Christ has done for men become mine?' by saying this: 'It becomes mine when I become part of this society, this fellowship, He left behind Him to be the continuation of His life on earth.' But obviously that answer raises further questions. How does one become a member of this society? Is it just a matter of joining a human organization? Does mere external membership in a Church guarantee my salvation? And if

[4] Gal. 2.20.   [7] Col. 3.1.   [10] I Cor. 1.30.
[5] Gal. 2.20.   [8] Eph. 2.6.
[6] Rom. 6.3.   [9] Phil. 3.9.

so, what has this to do with the death of Christ? We must look more closely at this society.

(b) Word, sacrament, prayer, fellowship

When we look at the outward marks of the fellowship which we see in the New Testament record, we shall find the following to be distinctive and outstanding. They are briefly summed up in a verse at the very beginning of Acts describing the first members of it. 'They continued steadfastly in the apostles' teaching and fellowship, in the breaking of bread and the prayers.'[11]

The first mark is the apostles' teaching. What that teaching was we know from the New Testament as a whole. It was the proclamation of what Jesus was and had done and would do. It is often spoken of simply as 'the Word', for in fact that proclamation had the same sort of creative power as did the Word of God on the day of creation.[12] This powerful Word, constantly sounding in the ears of those who gathered to hear it, bringing home to their hearts afresh the mighty acts which Jesus had done, brought the power of those acts—so to speak—to bear upon them ever afresh. That apostolic message was the foundation upon which their common life was built.

The second mark was the breaking of the bread. Jesus, knowing that words alone were not enough, had given to His disciples the simple ordinance of the Supper. Taking common bread and wine on the night of His passion, He had shared them with the disciples and told them: 'This is my body', 'This cup is the new covenant in my blood', and had bidden them take them in remembrance of Him. He wanted them to be not mere spectators of His passion,

[11] Acts 2.42.   [12] Gen. 1.1-3.

but (after His resurrection) to be taken up into it, made sharers in it. He alone could make the perfect offering to the Father for them; but the result of that should be that through Him they would also offer themselves in perfect penitence and obedience to the Father. This simple sacrament was to be the sign and means whereby they should do this. In St Paul's words it was 'a participation in the body and blood of Christ'.[13] So also, as He gave them this sacrament for their continual strengthening of their fellowship with Him, He gave them baptism as the sign, means and seal of their identification with Him in His death and resurrection for men. As He, in His acceptance of the baptism of repentance for sins, identified Himself with men, and accepted the cross, so He invited those who believed Him to be baptized into Him, not a mere sign of cleansing, but, henceforth, a sign and means of union with Him in His death and resurrection for men.

The third mark was fellowship. Not only by word and sacraments but by a new quality of common fellowship, in which each one was always building up the other in love, Jesus was continuing His ministry on earth of reconciling men to God. The authority to forgive sins which He had exercised in His ministry was exercised now in and through the life of a fellowship which was centred in Him and His atoning work. Because in His death sin had been both judged and forgiven, there was possible a fellowship among men in which it could be dealt with neither by evasion nor by self-righteous condemnation, but by mutual forgiveness.

The fourth mark was prayer—prayer offered in the confidence that comes from knowing that our great High

[13] I. Cor. 10.16.

Priest Jesus has entered on our behalf into the Holy Place
and that He ever lives to make intercession for us. This
kind of prayer is based upon what Jesus has done and
promised. It is part of the response of the believing fellowship to His self-offering.

These four visible marks are four links by which the
continuing fellowship is bound to Christ and His work,
continually renewed and re-directed by Him. And yet in
saying this we have still not reached the heart of the
matter. Preaching may become mere empty talk; sacraments may be perverted into empty symbol or pagan
magic; fellowship may give place to mere gregariousness
or to soulless organization; prayers may become lifeless
incantations. These things do not in themselves ensure
our participation in Christ; they are flesh, and flesh,
without spirit, is dead. 'It is the Spirit which quickeneth.'[14]
The union of the believer with Christ is the work of the
Spirit, quickening and using these visible means which
Christ has given to His people.

(c) The work of the Spirit

In the Old Testament we read of men who were given
special gifts of the Holy Spirit for special needs and times.
But the pouring out of the Spirit of God upon all men was
something which could not be expected until the 'last
days'.[15] Only in Jesus, the Beloved Son, did the Spirit dwell
in fulness and continuously. Jesus did not speak much of
the Spirit in the days of His ministry. The reason is stated
by St John: 'The Spirit was not yet given because Jesus
was not yet glorified.'[16] The Spirit could only be given
when Jesus had completed His work of atonement, when
He had provided the ransom, the sacrifice whereby sinful
men could come near to Holy God. Until He had done

[14] John 6.63.　　　[15] Joel 2.28.　　　[16] John 7.39.

that, there could be no union between God and man, and therefore no sharing for man in God's Spirit.

The New Testament record tells us that when Jesus had completed all his work on earth, convinced the disciples of the truth of His resurrection and of the meaning of His death, and withdrawn Himself from their sight and touch; after a short time of earnest prayer in fellowship the Holy Spirit was given to them. From the day of Pentecost onward the same Spirit who had been in Jesus was in them. By Him they were empowered to do the same mighty works which Jesus had done, and to preach boldly the good news of the kingdom of God. Moreover, because they were all sharers in the one Spirit, they were bound together like the limbs of one body. Their life was a common life; their possession of the Spirit was a shared possession. They were 'in Christ', members of His Body.

It is this supernatural gift of the Holy Spirit which unites believers with Christ, and makes them sharers in what He has done. But when we have said this we have still not fully explained the matter. For we have spoken of these things from the outside. We have looked at the first apostles and the Christians of the New Testament as though we were merely spectators. We cannot understand these things until we look at them from the inside. And in order to do that we must speak about faith. If we ask: What is it that unites us with Christ and makes us sharers in what He has done, we can answer in two ways: From God's side the answer is: It is the Holy Spirit who unites us with Christ; from man's side the answer is: It is faith which unites us with Christ. What is this faith?

(d) Faith

We have tried in the preceding chapter to understand what it was that happened when Christ Jesus was cruci-

D

fied. What happens to us when we understand that? We understand, in the first place, the enormity of our sin. In the presence of the Crucified, we and the whole human race are found to be guilty of treason against God. Apart from Christ we do not understand our sin in its full dimension. We make excuses for ourselves, compare ourselves with others, flatter ourselves that, although we are not perfect, we are better than some. In the presence of the cross we see what our sin is, and what it costs God.

In the second place, at the cross we understand the infinite depths of God's love. It is against God that we have sinned. And because God is Holy, He punishes sin and resists the onslaught of evil. It is of His ordinance that the wages of sin is death. But in His love for us sinners He has come down to bear upon Himself the burden of sin, to receive the wages of sin, to suffer the dread penalties of sin. The climax of His atoning work is to be seen in the words: 'My God, my God, why hast thou forsaken me?' There we see the Holy One of God bereft of God for man's sake. At the moment when He completely identified Himself with sinful men, dying between two criminals the shameful death of a criminal, and feeling in His own soul the terrible gulf which separates sinful men from God, He felt Himself on our side of the gulf, numbered with the transgressors, and enduring all the agony of separation from God as no sinner can ever endure it.

When we see and understand these things, we understand both God's judgment and God's mercy. We are humbled to the dust, and at the same time raised up and comforted. As we see the horror of our sin brought home to the loving heart of God, we cry: 'How hateful I must be to God! Surely I am fit only for death'. And at the same moment as we see Him deliberately bearing it all for our sake, standing on our side of the gulf, willing rather to be separated from the Father than to be separated from us, we cry in amazement: 'How precious I must be to God! Surely He who has done this for me, will never let me perish'. This double confession is something which is wrung from us by Christ's death. It is not that by an act of will I have decided to choose Christ as my saviour. It is that Christ has laid hold of me with this tremendous judgment and mercy and I am forced to cry out in shame and wondering gratitude: 'Lord, I am a traitor fit to die; Lord, thou hast died for me, and I am thine for ever'. This faith is, thus, wholly the result of what God has first done for me. It is not *first* an act of my will—that corrupted will which is always seeking something for itself instead of seeking the glory of God. It is, so to say, the 'Amen' which is wrung from my heart by this mighty act of Christ. It is the surrender of my will to Him, who alone can make my will free.

That surrender, that 'Amen', is faith. And it is the work of the Holy Spirit. We cannot separate these two. From God's side, it is the work of the Spirit; from my side it is faith. Yet that faith itself is not my independent work; it is the work of the Holy Spirit in my heart. Only God Himself has the power to bring my stubborn and rebellious will to the point of surrender. So that we must say that faith is the work of the Holy Spirit. And yet at the same time we ought also to say that it is through faith in Christ's work that we receive the Holy Spirit. It is when the cross of Christ has shattered our self-sufficiency, humbled our pride, and raised us again from the dust by the power of His love—only when this has been done that the Spirit of God can flow into our souls and take control of us. While the fortress-wall of self-righteousness remains standing, God's Holy Spirit cannot flow in.

Therefore we have to think always of these two things

together—faith and the Holy Spirit, and of both of them only through the work of Christ on the cross. The Spirit brings home to our hearts what Christ has done for us, and awakens that response which is faith—the Amen of the soul to God's judgment and God's mercy. That humble response places the soul in the position where the life-giving stream of God's Holy Spirit can flow in to possess the whole soul. The Spirit creates faith, and faith receives the Spirit. But all this is only through what Christ has accomplished on Calvary; the Spirit brings home to our hearts what Christ has done for us, through the preaching of the word of the Gospel, through the sacraments of baptism and the Lord's Supper, which He ordained, through the fellowship of His people, and through the prayers which they offer in His Name.

It is by these strong and many-stranded bonds that Christ unites us to Himself and makes us sharers in what He has done. Each of them depends intimately upon the other. Faith in Christ is born in us when the fact of His crucifixion is brought home to us in word and sacrament, through the power of the Spirit. The continuing fellow-ship of His people from the day of Pentecost, till the day of His coming again, lives by the apostolic teaching and fellowship, the breaking of bread, and prayer; but these things depend for their life upon the quickening work of the Spirit, and they become the means of uniting us with Christ through faith. The Spirit, working in and through this continuing fellowship and its various means of grace, both creates faith and also is known and received through faith. Thus by faith, in the Church, and in the Spirit we are made partakers of Christ.

(e) Regeneration

In speaking of what happens when we understand the

cross, we have used such terms as 'shattering and upbuild-
ing', 'dying and living'. The cross is God's death-sentence
upon human sin, and at the same time it is the gift of new
life. Before the cross a man is driven to say, like Paul: 'I
am dead; yet I live, yet not I, but Christ lives in me'.[17]
The cross is the place where men are dead and made alive
again.

This tremendous experience is described in many parts
of the New Testament as 'being born again'. Thus Peter
speaks of Christians as having been 'begotten again not of
corruptible seed, but of incorruptible, through the word
of God'.[18] Our Lord Himself tells Nicodemus that a man
cannot see the kingdom of God unless he is born again,
and there are many other cases where He says that it is
necessary to become again as a little child. In the first
chapter of St. John's Gospel there is this very important
passage: 'As many as received him, to them gave he the
right to become children of God, even to them that believe
on his name, which were born not of blood nor of the will
of the flesh nor of the will of man, but of God'.[19] The
same contrast between the new birth and birth 'according
to the flesh' is made in the talk with Nicodemus.[20] Birth
'according to the flesh' is ordinary human birth. It is the
beginning of ordinary human life under the conditions of
sin which we have spoken about in the second chapter.
The new birth is that new kind of life which is the work
of the Holy Spirit in him who has faith in Christ. Only
this new life can bring forth the kind of fruits that God
wants. As Jesus Himself said: 'A good tree cannot bring
forth evil fruit, neither can a corrupt tree bring forth good
fruit'.[21] It is by the creation of a new nature in us, by a

[17] Gal. 2.20.
[18] I Peter 1.23.
[19] John 1.12-13.
[20] John 3.6.
[21] Matt. 7.18.

new birth through the death of Christ, that we are enabled to do what is pleasing to God. We have seen how this new birth takes place. When through the work of the Holy Spirit, in the life, word, sacraments and prayer of the Church, the dying of Christ is brought home to my heart and received in faith, a new mind is created in me. My ordinary human nature is brought under a death sentence; but death is not the end, for He died that I might live, and His dying for me brings forth a new life in me, a life which is lived 'in Christ' and 'for Christ'. It is from that new birth that the good deeds of the Christian life spring. They come from a new heart, a new will, created and energized by the love of God in Christ. They are the response of gratitude to His infinite love. They are good fruit, because they come from a new, good tree—from Jesus Himself the true Vine.

It is necessary here to make a very important qualification of what has been written above. We have been speaking of the fully conscious experience of such men as St Paul. And in order to understand regeneration rightly it is necessary that we should approach it in this way. But we must also remember that the regenerating work of the Holy Spirit is something greater and more mysterious than we can fully understand and express. Even the greatest Christian cannot fully experience or express all that the Holy Spirit has done in him to recreate him into the true image of God—a child of God through Jesus Christ. We should always try to enter as far as we can into the full experience of, and understanding of our regeneration. But the work of the Holy Spirit through word and sacrament, through the prayers and fellowship of the Church, does not simply depend upon our understanding of it. In the practice of infant baptism the Church has a perpetual reminder of this fact. The work of God the Holy Spirit in recreating us as children of God begins even before we have any conscious understanding of it. Christians are not all agreed about the nature of baptism —how far it is simply a declaration of the new birth, and how far it is also the means which the Holy Spirit works in us. We can never fully understand how this regenerating work is done, but it is our task to seek more and more to understand it, to yield ourselves consciously to Him, and so to allow Him to bring to full stature the new nature which He has given us.

It is also important to remember that, even though the Christian life is truly the result of a new birth, yet, nevertheless, the old person still exists. That old human person, who was judged and condemned to death at the cross, still exists. He has to be put to death again every day. The new birth is not finished and done with—not until the day of Christ's coming. So there is a warfare every day for the Christian between the old man and the new, between the flesh and the Spirit. Even though we have put off the old man and put on the new, yet we have to do this afresh every day. This is made very clear by St Paul.[22] When he speaks of a warfare between flesh and Spirit[23] he does not mean a warfare between our minds and our bodies; he means a warfare between that old man with his ordinary human nature, 'born of the flesh', which was condemned at the cross, and the new man, 'born of the Spirit', which was created in us by the love of Christ.

This warfare is painful. We often wish that it could cease, and we wonder why the old man should continue to live and trouble us. The answer to this is that God has deliberately left us still bound up in the bundle of life with all men, sharing the same ordinary human nature with others, because he wants the saving power of Christ

[22] e.g. Col. 3.1-17.   [23] e.g. Gal. 5.17.

to do its work throughout the whole world and in all men. He wants to redeem the whole world, and therefore He does not take us out of the world, but leaves us here to carry on the good fight of faith. And that fight is chiefly a fight within ourselves to put off the old man every day and put on the new man—to stand before the cross and crucify the old man so that the new man may be re-born daily in love and gratitude, to bring forth loving deeds in the power of the Spirit.

(f) Justification

The problem with which we started, the problem with which God has to deal in order to bring about salvation, is the problem of sin. Sin means that man is cut off from the true source of his being in God; instead of loving, trusting and obeying God, he loves himself, distrusts God, and tries to be his own master. We have seen that man cannot save himself from this situation. His will has been thoroughly corrupted, and even when he wills salvation, he wills it for himself. Even when he wills to be righteous, it leads him to a selfish sort of righteousness which cuts him off from the love of God and man. And equally God cannot solve the problem by simply wiping out man's sin as though it did not exist. If God did not resist and punish sin, the world would become a hell. Yet God's punishment of sin, the wrath with which He withstands sin, does not and cannot bring about salvation.

We have seen that the mighty act of Jesus in dying on the cross reveals both God's judgment upon sin and also His mercy. It reveals both the awful character of sin, and the terrible punishment which it brings, and at the same time it shows us God bearing all the punishment upon His own heart for our sake. And when man, through the work of the Holy Spirit, understands and believes that, then he knows himself both judged and forgiven. He knows himself a fit object only for God's wrath, and yet the object of God's love. In other words, there is in his heart an echo of what was in Christ's heart—an acceptance of and submission to God's just judgment of his sin, and commitment of himself to God's love. It is only through the sufferings of the sinless One that the sinful can understand what their sin means and accept God's judgment upon it. And it is those sufferings which enable him to commit himself wholly to God's love, because behind the wrath of God he sees the love of God going to the last limit to save the sinner.

A man who, through the work of the Holy Spirit, understands and believes this, is therefore put into the right relation with God. He begins to have that mind towards the Father which Christ had. Christ's mind is formed in him. As Christ has put Himself in the sinner's place before the Father, so the sinner—understanding and believing what has been done—finds himself looking to the Father with the mind of Christ—that is, in humble penitence and love. That believing, obeying, loving mind towards God is righteousness. It is the only true righteousness. True righteousness is not a possession of my own which I can have apart from God; that is self-righteousness, and it is the very essence of sin. True righteousness is a relation of loving trust and obedience towards God. At the beginning of our study we saw that unbelief is the root of sin. So now we have to say that faith is the essence of righteousness. By His dying for sinners, with sinners, in the place of sinners, Christ has made it possible for sinners to have that mind towards God; and that mind is righteousness. It is what Paul calls 'the righteousness which is of God by faith'.[24]

[24] Phil. 3.9.

In St Paul's Epistles, especially Romans and Galatians, but also in others, much time is given to the explanation of this 'righteousness which is of God by faith', and the contrast between it and 'the righteousness of the law'. But the same difference is very simply portrayed in two of Jesus' parables. In one[25] he describes two men praying in the Temple. One, a Pharisee, thanked God for his own good deeds; the other, a publican, simply stood with bowed head and said: 'God be merciful to me a sinner'. And Jesus said that it was the publican and not the Pharisee whom God accepted as a righteous man. If we think of righteousness as a possession of our own, then certainly the Pharisee was more righteous than the publican. His own list of virtues is enough to prove that. But this is not true righteousness, because it is centred in the self and not in God, and therefore it is without love. In fact such so-called 'righteousness' is the very essence of sin; it is the most extreme form of man's attempt to be like God.[26] That was proved when the Pharisees, the religious leaders of the time, took the lead in crucifying Jesus. Probably the publican was guilty of breaking most of the ten commandments. He did not even dare to lift up his eyes in the Temple. He could only cast himself utterly on the love of God. And Jesus says: 'He went home justified'. That does not mean that he had been suddenly transformed into a good Pharisee; it means that he was in the right relationship to God.

The other story is even better known. We call it 'The Prodigal Son', but the proper name for it is 'The Two Sons'. If you read the whole chapter you will see that the reason for which Jesus told it was that the Pharisees were murmuring against Him for His close association with sinners.[27] The elder son never left his father's house, and

[25] Luke 18.9-14.   [26] Gen. 3.5.   [27] Luke 15.1-2.

never transgressed his commandments.[28] But at the end he was left outside the father's house—not of the father's will, but of his own. The father went out to entreat him to come in, but he would not. He thought that his status in the father's house was his right, that he had earned it by his hard work. Therefore he could not share his father's joy when the bad son came home. The younger son had shamefully betrayed his father's good name and wasted his goods. He knew that he had no right to be in his father's house. He did not claim any rights. He simply cast himself on his father's love. And at once he was taken in as a beloved son, given the ring and the robe and the fatted calf. At the end of the story Jesus leaves this unforgettable picture on our minds: the younger son who has deserved nothing is in the father's home, and surrounded by love and joy; the elder son who believes that he deserves everything is left outside—even though the father pleads with him to come in. That is a picture of the two kinds of righteousness—what Paul calls 'the righteousness of God by faith', and 'the righteousness which is of the law'; the faith-righteousness which is all God's gift, and the self-righteousness which a man tries to have as his own possession. The former takes us into the very presence of God; the latter finally shuts us out. What Paul is saying again and again in his Epistles is this: you must choose between these two kinds of righteousness, and you cannot possibly have both. You cannot be both a coolie and a son. You cannot both earn God's favour as a right, like a workman earning his wages, and also enjoy His love like a son in his father's home. If you want to have a righteousness of your own, the righteousness which comes by law, then you are certainly shut out of the righteousness of God, that which is by grace.

[28] Luke 15.29.

The pious Jews had longed and prayed for the day when God would appear and His righteousness be made manifest. In spite of all the wickedness of the world, the successes of the wicked and the sufferings of the good, they continued to believe that there was a righteous God in heaven, and that He would surely come to judge the earth. Then those who had faithfully kept the Law of God would be pronounced righteous, and those who had flouted it would be condemned.

This is the proper meaning of the word 'justify'. It is the opposite of the word 'condemn'. It does not refer to a process by which a man is changed inwardly from a bad man into a good man. It refers to the sentence of a judge by which a man is pronounced to be in the right. In Jewish thought (as in any ordinary human thought) a just judge is one who justifies the righteous and condemns the ungodly. It was a terrible scandal to the Jews to hear Christians preaching that God is one who justifies the ungodly.[29] Yet this is the very heart of the Gospel. Jesus Himself gave expression to it when He said: 'I came not to call the righteous, but sinners'.[30]

Every earnest Jew laboured so to keep the Law of God that on that day he would be 'justified', that is, declared by the judge to be in the right. The Gospel is a complete reversal of this expectation. There are no 'righteous'. All are found guilty. But the righteous judge, when He came for judgment, Himself took the place of the sinner in order that the sinners might be put in the right. And we have seen how this happens. When a man understands and believes what Jesus has done for him, a new mind is formed in him. He 'comes to himself', recognizes the truth, realizes his sin for what it is, and casts himself utterly on God's mercy. And that man is immediately 'put

[29] Rom. 4.5.   [30] Matt. 9.13.

right with God'. Like the prodigal son he is immediately taken right into the Father's heart. He is given all the privileges of a beloved son. He is not put on probation to see whether his new disposition will last. He is taken in just as he is. That is what the New Testament means by 'justification'. The prodigal son was not suddenly changed in nature. He is still the same person. But he is put into a new relation with the Father; he becomes part of the Father's household, living in intimate fellowship and love with the Father.

It is out of this act of God in taking the sinner to Himself that the good deeds of the Christian life flow. He does not do good deeds in order to earn eternal life. That is the motive of the Pharisees, and because it is fundamentally selfish it is also loveless. No, the Christian does good because he *has been given* eternal life. He has been taken into the Father's home, when he deserved nothing but banishment and shame. And in love and gratitude he begins to live a new sort of life, the life which is suitable to such a home. The Father's love produces an answering love in him. He wants to behave in such a way as will please his Father—not in order that he may earn something, but because he has been given everything. His good deeds are an overflow from a heart which is brimfull of the Father's love. And these are real good deeds, because they are really loving. They do not arise from the selfish motive of trying to earn God's favour. They are a pure outflow of love. And so they have a sort of freedom and generosity which is lacking in any sort of legal system of righteousness. When the woman from the streets burst into the house of Simon the Pharisee[31] and poured out upon the feet of Jesus the most precious ointment that she had, she was not acting according to any code, or trying to

[31] Luke 7.36 ff.

earn any merit. She was simply trying to express her love
for Jesus, the love of a forgiven sinner for her Saviour.
And that is the true essence of all real goodness. It is the
free, spontaneous, uncalculating outflow of love from a
loving heart.

There is thus absolutely no place in the Christian life
for the idea of merit. It is not because of any good that
we do that we are accepted by God. There is no possibility
of earning His favour. If we have even a little of that
thought we shall find ourselves outside with the elder
brother, we shall find the feasting of heaven as unpleasant
as he found the feasting for the prodigal son. The greatest
saint cannot earn his place in God's home. We are there
simply because of His grace. We are ready to come in
there when we have the new mind that is created by
Christ's death, when we know, at the same moment,
how hateful we are to God, and how precious we are
to Him.

(g) Growth in holiness

When the prodigal son returns to his father's house he
is still covered with the rags of his poverty. His body is
diseased with evil living and emaciated with starvation.
His mind is polluted by the evil thoughts which have
occupied it for many years. His habits of life and speech
are those which he has learned from evil friends in the far
country. The father does not wait till these things have
been cleansed before he receives him. He runs out to him
and embraces him, brings him into the house. He does
not wait for him to be changed, but takes him as he is.

In one sense, everything is changed from that moment.
He is no longer a wastrel in a far country, he is a beloved
son in his father's house. And yet in another sense the
change can only come gradually. The body will not all at

once regain its strength and health. Those evil thoughts and habits will not all at once drop off. The change in his status will have to be gradually wrought out in every part of his life and thought and speech. He will have to learn gradually to master bad habits, to check evil speech, to drive out evil thoughts. Probably he will often slip, and he will know that he is wounding his dear father by words or deeds which are unfit for such a home. Probably at first he will not realize just what a tremendous change has to take place. Words and thoughts which seemed quite natural in that far country will slip out here, and he will see the pain in his father's eyes, and he will realize with a shock that such things cannot be done here. He will run to ask his father's pardon, and he will feel with a new intensity the greatness of the father's love, and his own utter unworthiness of it. It will only be by slow degrees that he will come to be so much one in thought and will and feelings with the father, that his thoughts and words quite naturally rise to the same level as his father's. And even to the end, he will never be able to forget that he is in the house only by his father's great kindness.

· But here even this parable breaks down. For the difference between even the best human father and the worst human son is a finite difference. But the difference between God and sinful man is infinite. Therefore all the saints will testify that the more we grow in grace, the more we feel the terrible contrast between our best goodness and God's holy love. Here we cannot help speaking in a paradox. Like the prodigal son, the Christian is given a completely new status. From the moment that he turns to God in faith through Jesus Christ, he is accepted as a beloved son. And yet it is only by slow degrees that the change in his status is to be wrought out in his whole being, so that his body, mind, and spirit become com-

pletely filled and controlled by the Spirit of God. There
has to be a process of growth, of daily warfare against
the evil tendencies which still exist in our human nature
(what the Bible calls our 'flesh'). Yet the difference
between man's best holiness and the holiness of God is
such that, even to the very end, an honest man must know
himself to be a sinner needing fresh repentance and fresh
forgiveness. Not once only, but every day, he has to say:
'I will arise and go to my father, and say, father, I have
sinned against heaven and in thy sight'.

Conversion is in one sense something which happens
once for all, but in another sense it is something which
has to happen daily afresh. The Christian, as Luther said,
is at the same time both a righteous man and a sinner. He
is accepted by God into the intimacy of His own home;
and yet at the same time he is still a sinner utterly unfit
for that home. To the day of his death and beyond it, that
will still be true. And yet that does not mean that we can
adopt an attitude of complacency towards our sins. It does
not mean that—since God forgives our sins—we can
afford not to worry too much about them. To the very
end we shall be unfit for our Father's home; and yet it is
surely unthinkable that we should be content to enjoy the
love of His home and constantly do things which wound
His heart. Just because we have been given sonship, we
have to strive daily to be true sons. And that means a warfare against the flesh, a daily putting to death of the old
self, and a daily putting on of the new self which is God's
gracious gift. The latter parts of most of St Paul's letters
are concerned with this aspect of the Christian life. And
in one of our Lord's parables we are reminded of how
terrible a thing it is to despise God's grace, like an
unworthy wedding guest who has been invited to a king's
feast, and given a wedding garment to cover his filthy

garments, but does not care to take the trouble to put it on.[32] Such a man, says our Lord, will be cast out into the darkness. So the apostle tells us, with many stern warnings, that just because we have been made new in Christ, we are to put off the old man 'and put on the new man which, after God, hath been created in righteousness and holiness of truth '.[33]

This putting on of the new man means first of all a constant participation in the life of the fellowship of God's children, and in the means of grace with which it has been furnished. By remaining in that fellowship, by hearing the word of the Gospel, by participation in the sacrament of the Lord's Supper, and by participation in the Church's life of prayer, we are brought again and again into the presence and power of God's saving acts through Jesus. In this way the mind of Christ is constantly renewed in us. That mind which is created in us by the power of the Holy Spirit in the presence of the cross, is constantly re-created as the cross is represented to us in Word and Sacrament. And in the prayers of the Church, in which we share both in public worship and in private prayer, all our life and the common life of mankind is brought within the sphere of working of Christ's atonement and subdued to His will.

Secondly, the extension of this life in Christ will be seen in the acts of witness and service by which we go out to bring all things under the power of Christ's atonement. God's purpose in Christ is nothing less than to sum up all things in Him.[34] Until that purpose is complete, His travail continues and our salvation is not complete. It is an essential part of our sonship that we should share in the travail of His soul,[35] and in the work and witness by

[32] Matt. 22.11-14.
[33] Eph. 4.22-24; Col. 3.1-17.
[34] Eph. 1.10.
[35] Isa. 53.11.

which Christ's atonement is to be brought to its consummation. Of this we shall speak in the next chapter.

Christian growth in holiness does not mean a striving
to climb up to the place where we may enjoy fellowship
with God. This is, in the first place, impossible, and in the
the second place the Christian Gospel is that God has come
down to where we sinful men are, in order to give us
fellowship with Himself here. That fellowship is given at
the mercy-seat where Christ has borne our sins. Christian
growth means the gradual working out in our own life
of what has been given to us. From first to last its motive
force is gratitude to our Redeemer. And its goal is not that
I should be saved, but that my Redeemer should 'see of
the travail of his soul and be satisfied'.[36]

[36] Isa. 53.11.

VIII

THE CONSUMMATION OF SALVATION

(a) The Christian hope

AT the beginning of this book we spoke of salvation as the summing up of all things in Christ, the healing of that which is broken, the restoring of the lost unity between man and God, man and man, and man and nature. That salvation still lies in the future. We still long for it. But we do not merely long for it; we also experience it now, in foretaste. The New Testament speaks often of the Holy Spirit as an *earnest* of the inheritance which is laid up for us.[1] That union which we have now with God and with one another through the Holy Spirit is a foretaste, an earnest of the perfect salvation which is to be ours. An earnest is not a complete possession. But it is a guarantee that the full possession will be ours. This guarantee has been given to us in the Holy Spirit. We do not have complete possession of our inheritance. We still have to fight against sin; the Spirit has to war against the flesh. Sometimes we may be driven almost to despair. But because we have been given the earnest, we are sure that we shall receive in due time the full inheritance.

God has given us another kind of assurance also, in the resurrection of Jesus from the dead. Paul calls Him 'the first fruits of them that sleep', and argues that by His resurrection we are given assurance about our own.[2]

[1] II Cor. 1.22; 5.5; Eph. 1.14.   [2] I Cor. 15.

Similarly Peter says that the resurrection of Jesus has caused us to be 'born again to a living hope' for the inheritance laid up for us.[3] The resurrection of Jesus, and the gift of the Holy Spirit, provide us with an unshakable assurance, outward and inward, that our hope of the kingdom of God is not a dream, but is based upon God's sure promise.

Hope is thus an essential part of the Christian life, and is often spoken of as such in the New Testament. This hope is not a mere desire for something uncertain. It is a joyful assurance about the completion of God's saving work in Christ. As believers in Him we live in the midst of that saving work. Through the death and resurrection of Jesus we have been brought to repentance and rebirth as God's children, and we live in the fellowship of His Spirit. And yet we still also live in the world. Our 'old man' remains. We are all part and parcel of this world which is still under the power of sin and death. So we have a sort of double existence. We taste salvation even now. But we cannot have it fully until God's work is completed. For it is His purpose to save the world. He does not want to take out of the world a few individuals who selfishly wish for their own happiness. He loves the world and longs for its salvation; and therefore those who have received His Spirit will also share this love and longing. So St Paul says: 'We know that the whole creation groaneth and travaileth in pain together until now; and not only so, but ourselves also, which have the first-fruits of the Spirit, even we ourselves groan within ourselves, waiting for our adoption, to wit the redemption of our body'.[4] It is part of our Christian life that we long for and hope and pray for and work for the consummation of His saving purpose for the whole world. Therefore also in

[3] I Peter 1.3-5.   [4] Rom. 8.22-23.

our Communion Service,[5] we say: 'Thy death, O Lord, we commemorate; thy resurrection we confess: and thy second coming we await'. The Church lives in that spirit —both having and hoping for salvation.

(b) The coming again of Christ

What exactly do we hope for? The centre of our hope is nothing other than Christ Himself. We cannot hope for anything apart from Him. It is in Him that we have received the revelation of God, have been judged, forgiven and born again. For the present He is removed from the reach of our sight or touch. We know Him through the Spirit but that knowledge is only partial and dim.[6] It is only a foretaste of what He wills for us. What we long for is that we should see Him as He is. But that can only be possible to us when we are like Him.[7] We know now that we are His and He is ours, but that unity is not complete; there is still much in us which is at enmity with Him, and there is much in Him which is not yet ours. We long for perfect union with Him. But that union can only come for us as it comes for all who are His. Therefore what we long for is the day when His love has won its full victory, and all things are enfolded and made one in Him.

Of course when we speak of these things we have to speak in pictures, because we are speaking of things which no man has seen or can see.[8] We have no other language that we can use. But the picture is not merely produced out of our imagination. The centre of the picture is Jesus, and He is not a product of our imagination. He has promised that He will come again, that He will draw all men to Himself. His love will in the end be victorious. That

[5] Liturgy of the Church of South India.
[6] I Cor. 13.12.
[7] I John 3.2.
[8] I Cor. 2.9.

is the point to which we look forward in hope. And we know that this hope cannot be disappointed because God has given us His Holy Spirit as the pledge of its fulfilment.[9]

(c) *Judgment*

The Apostles' Creed reminds us that, when He comes again, it will be 'to judge the quick and the dead'. We have seen that Christ's work on the cross is both a work of judgment and a work of mercy. It manifests at the same time God's wrath and God's love, God's condemnation of the sinner and God's saving love for the sinner. We have also seen that it is only because of this double character of Christ's death on the cross that it is the means of salvation for us. It saves us, because it brings us to a true penitence and a true faith. In its light, the lies created by sin are dispelled, and we see our sin as it truly is, and God's love as it truly is. Without judgment there can be no salvation from sin, for without judgment there can be no righteousness.

In the cross God's judgment and His salvation are revealed, but they are not fully consummated. It is there revealed that the whole human race is under the condemnation of God's holiness. But God has not carried out that sentence of condemnation. He holds it back, so to say, in order to give men time to repent. He sends out His Church to tell all men the gospel, in order that they may repent and be saved. His will is that all should be saved. He does not will the destruction of any soul. Some Christians have taught that God created some men for the purpose of destroying them, but that is quite false teaching. It is based upon a misunderstanding of certain passages in Scripture, but it is certainly not the teaching of the Gospel.

[9] Rom. 5.5.

If God wills that all should be saved, does that mean that all will be saved? We cannot say that. We know that God has given men freedom to choose good or evil. We cannot say that it is impossible that men should finally choose evil. Christ has given us many terrible parables in which we have a picture of men finally cast out of the light and love of home into the outer darkness. He has also used the name Gehenna to describe this final destruction. Gehenna was the name of the valley where the rubbish and filth of Jerusalem was deposited. It was a place where there were always fires burning. It was a symbol to Him of the possibility of men becoming finally useless and fit only for burning. We cannot exclude this possibility from our minds, if we wish to remain true to His mind.

The disciples once asked Jesus: 'Lord, are they few that be saved?'[10] Jesus answered: 'Strive to enter in by the narrow door, for many, I say unto you, shall seek to enter in and shall not be able'. Jesus does not answer our theoretical questions about Hell. But He bids us recognize that the door into life is narrow, and that it is possible, and indeed terribly easy to miss it. In the end this is certain: that what opposes the love of God must be done away. We believe that God wills to knit together all His created world in one common salvation, in which the glory of His love will be perfectly revealed and reflected. We have seen in Jesus that this involves a judgment upon the whole human race as it is now. We know that He has given time for men to hear and believe the gospel, to repent, and to return to Him. But at the end we cannot deny the possibility that men—even the majority of men —may be left outside. If they are left outside, it will be because—like the elder brother in the parable—they are not willing to share the Father's fellowship on His terms.

[10] Luke 13.23.

His invitation is to everyone. 'He that cometh unto me I will in no wise cast out.'[11] But when we begin to speculate about the question of eternal loss we are quickly in regions where we do not know the answer. We can only give heed to the words of our Lord: 'Strive to enter in by the narrow door'.

(d) Resurrection

When we speak about a final salvation and a final judgment in which all are to share, we are assuming that death is not the end of human life. But this is a very big assumption to make, and we must ask whether it is justified, and what we believe about what lies beyond death. For, as far as our own human experience is concerned, death appears to be a full-stop which puts an end to the human story. Of course if this were so, there could be no talk about salvation. Human life would be a meaningless tale, without purpose and without value.

Almost all men at all times have had some sort of belief about existence beyond death. In India the dominant belief is that after death the soul is born again in another body, whether human, bestial, or celestial, according to its *Karma*. Among many ancient peoples, and among the Jews of the Old Testament, it was believed that after death men's souls went to a Sheol, a place of dim shadowy existence without purpose and without meaning. The Jews of early days, when they spoke of God's coming kingdom, thought of a kingdom of this earth and on this side of death. It is true that there are wonderful passages in the Old Testament in which we see faith in the living God leading on to assurance that He is able to deliver the soul from Sheol and to give to His people 'pleasures for evermore' at His right hand.[12] Nevertheless

[11] John 6.37.   [12] Ps. 16.

it is clear that in the main the Jews of the Old Testament looked for 'the goodness of the Lord in the land of the living'.[13] They believed that God's holiness would be vindicated and His kingdom established on earth, with Jerusalem as its capital. But in later ages, especially after the terrible persecutions which they underwent at the hands of Greek and Roman empires, they found it difficult to believe that all the glories of God's kingdom should be reserved for those who happened to be living at that time, while those who had shed their blood as martyrs for the kingdom should be shut out. Many therefore came to believe in the possibility of a resurrection, by which the heroes of faith of olden age would be able to share in the glories of the coming kingdom. In the time of our Lord the Pharisees held this belief, but the more conservative Sadducees denied it.[14]

In this matter the first Christians found themselves on the same side as the Pharisees, but of course with one enormous difference. Their assurance about resurrection was based upon the resurrection of Jesus. That amazing fact was the starting point of the Christian preaching. Jesus, whom they had seen taken out to His death and buried in the tomb of Joseph, had on the third day risen from the dead, left behind an empty tomb, and appeared to them in all the glory of a new creation. This could only mean that the new age, the last days for which holy men had longed and prayed, had actually dawned. In the light of this fact, the events of Jesus' life, death and ministry were interpreted as the beginning of the 'last things' to which the prophets had looked forward. The kingdom of God had actually arrived on the threshold. And this of course is exactly what Jesus had said at the beginning of His ministry.[15] The healing miracles of Jesus were the sign

[13] Ps. 27.13. [14] Acts 23.8; Luke 20.27. [15] Mark 1.14.

that the 'last days' foretold by prophets had come.[16] His death was the revelation of God's final judgment; His resurrection was the 'first fruit'[17] to prove that the final harvest was near; and the coming of the Holy Spirit was the fulfilment of Joel's prophecy about the 'last days'.[18] In all these things the believers found evidence that through Christ they had been brought to a foretaste of the coming kingdom of God. They were already sharers in it. And the foretaste made them sure about the completion. As God had raised Jesus from the dead, so He would certainly raise up those who are Christ's at His coming.[19] The whole Body of Christ is one fellowship, and the whole body shall at the end be raised up to share in the glory which the disciples saw in the risen body of Jesus.

The New Testament thus speaks more about the resurrection of the body than about the immortality of the soul. We are not told very much about what happens to the souls of men when they die. St Paul clearly believed that at death he would go to be with Christ.[20] But at other times he speaks of those who have died as being 'asleep' and waiting for the day of resurrection to awake them.[21] What is quite clear is that the first Christians were looking forward with longing to the day of Christ's return, and that they understood this to include the resurrection of those who were His. This point is a very important one. If we speak only of the immortality of the soul, and if we think only (as many Christians do) of going to heaven when we die, we have forgotten the most important part of the Christian hope. We have again become selfish individualists. What God longs for, and what we must long

---

[16] Cf. Matt. 12.15-21.
[17] I Cor. 15.20.
[18] Acts 2.14-21.
[19] I Cor. 15.20-23.
[20] Phil. 1.21-24.
[21] I Thess. 4.13-18; I Cor. 15.18.

for, is the salvation of the world. And that must mean the resurrection of the whole body of Christ, which includes all who are His true members. This raises difficult questions to which we cannot give a certain answer. The Corinthians asked Paul 'How are the dead raised and with what manner of body do they come?'[22] Paul in his answer uses the simile of a grain of wheat, which falls into the ground and dies, and God brings a sort of new creation out of it.[23] It is the same seed, and yet it is something new. Of course we are here passing beyond the bounds of human knowledge and can only speak in parables. What is clear is that 'flesh and blood cannot inherit the kingdom of God'.[24] This old man which we have to be continually putting to death by the power of the Spirit has finally to be put in the grave and left to rot. But there is a new man which God is creating. Even now we know something of it. And on that day it will be complete and perfect—a new man, a new body, a new creation.[25] This new man is Christ Himself, in whom we are all to be members.

But this new creation involves not only our souls and bodies, it also involves the whole created world. None of God's creation is irrelevant to His purpose. None of it is mere scaffolding to be thrown away when the building is complete. He made it all in love, and He loves it all. Therefore the completion of His purpose means not only the resurrection, but also a new heaven and a new earth. There are glimpses of this in the Old Testament.[26] In the New Testament it comes to its most vivid fulfilment in the visions of the Book of Revelations about the new Jerusalem, and of this we shall speak now.

[22] I Cor. 15.35.
[23] I. Cor. 15.36-38, 42-46.
[24] I Cor. 15.50.
[25] See II Cor. 4.16-5.4.
[26] e.g. Isa. 11.6-9; 35.1-7; 65.17.

(e) The kingdom of God

The New Testament ends with a glowing picture which is familiar to us all: 'I saw a new heaven and a new earth for the first heaven and the first earth are passed away, and the sea is no more. And I saw the holy city, new Jerusalem, coming down out of heaven from God made ready as a bride adorned for her husband. And I heard a great voice out of the throne saying, Behold the tabernacle of God is with men and he shall dwell with them and they shall be his peoples and God himself shall dwell with them and be their God; and he shall wipe away every tear from their eyes, and death shall be no more; neither shall there be mourning, nor crying, nor pain, any more: the first things are passed away. And he that sitteth upon the throne said, Behold, I make all things new.'[27]

The atonement which Christ has wrought between God and men has as its ultimate goal this new creation, in which all things are re-created in Him. It is to be noted that the final picture is not of a church but of a city. In fact it is definitely said that there is no temple there, 'for the Lord God the Almighty and the Lamb are the temple thereof'.[28] God's purpose is not to create a little group of people separated from the world; it is to create the world anew through Christ. For that purpose He has sent His Son to make atonement for the sins of the world and to reconcile men to Himself. His Church is the body which He has formed to continue that work until its consummation.

Of that consummation the Bible speaks in many glowing pictures. If we are to describe it in a few words we can only say this: it is the restoration of creation to its original purpose by the purging away of sin. It is the

[27] Rev. 21.1-5.　　[28] Rev. 21.22.

restoring of all men and all things to perfect harmony and perfect joy, through the perfect love of God.

For that consummation we wait in eager hope. We know that He has promised it and that He is faithful. We know also that He has called us to be His witnesses and servants in bringing the whole world under obedience to His holy will. We are not called by Christ simply that we ourselves may be saved: we are called in order to be partners in His saving work. His invitation is to all men. If we are not willing to join Him in inviting all men to share it; if we are content to have His love for ourselves and do not wish to share it with all, then at the end—like the elder brother—we shall be left outside. But if we have understood His love, if we have tasted His grace, that foretaste will make us eager to share with Him in the pain and sorrow of the world's redemption, in eager and confident hope of the day when we and all His people shall enter into His joy together, and He shall see of the travail of His soul and be satisfied.

INDEX OF BIBLICAL REFERENCES

(The figures printed in italics refer to page numbers in the book)

OLD TESTAMENT

GENESIS

1.1-3	*94*
1.26-27	*16*
2.7-17	*18*
2.16-17	*19*
ch. 3	*37*
3.1-6	*19*
3.5	*20, 106*
3.7-4.15	*21*
3.9-10	*22*
3.12-13	*21*
3.16	*21*
3.17-19	*21*
3.23-24	*21*
4.1-15	*22*
12.1-3	*46*
22.1-13	*86*

EXODUS

24.4-11	*67*

LEVITICUS

19.18	*48*
25.47-55	*80*

JUDGES

21.25	*52*

I SAMUEL

8.7 ff.	*52*
9.15-16	*52*

PSALMS

16	*120*
27.13	*121*
49.7-8	*66*
51.2-3	*34*
51.3	*34*
51.4	*34, 36*
93	*32*
104	*32*

ISAIAH

5.1-7	*65*
11.1-12	*53*
11.6-9	*123*
35.1-7	*123*
41.14	*80*
43.1	*80*
44.6	*80*
47.4	*80*
52.13-53.12	*54*
ch. 53	*63*
53.6	*77*
53.10-12	*84*
53.11	*113, 114*
60.16	*80*
65.17	*123*

JOEL

2.28	*96*

MICAH

6.6-8	*47*

NEW TESTAMENT

MATTHEW

4.8-10	*53*
7.18	*24, 101*
9.13	*108*
10.39	*59*
12.15-21	*122*
12.35-36	*24*

MATTHEW (cont.)

18.6	*76*
22.11-14	*113*
23.23	*48*
26.28	*66*
26.40	*68*

MARK

1.4	*64*
1.9-11	*84*
1.10	*64*
1.11	*64*
1.14	*121*
2.7	*70*

MARK (*cont.*)

2.19-20	62
3.1-6	63
7.21-23	24
8.31	63
8.33	89
8.34	68
8.35	67, 68
8.38	59
9.12	63
9.31	63
10.33-34	63
10.45	66, 81
12.1-9	65, 75
12.6	59 f.
14.24	66
14.36	63
14.58	68
15.29	68
15.34	64

LUKE

7.36 ff.	109 f.
9.51	63, 89
10.18	88
11.20-22	88
12.50	64
13.23	119
15.1-2	106
15.29	107
18.9-14	106
20.18	65
20.27	121
22.37	63
23.39	79
23.39-43	78
23.41	78
24.25-27	90 f.

JOHN

1.12-13	101

JOHN (*cont.*)

1.14	58
2.19-22	68
3.6	101
3.16	56 ff.
3.19	74
4.14	61
4.22	45
5.19	71
ch. 6	67
6.15	53
6.37	120
6.63	96
7.39	96
9.1-7	39
9.39-41	27
10.10-11	67
10.18	71
12.24-25	67
12.31	88
12.32	67
13.1	71
18.11	53
18.36	53

ACTS

2.14-21	122
2.24	90
2.42	94

ROMANS

1.18	27, 41
1.18-32	27
1.22 f.	28 f.
1.24	41
1.24-27	28 f.
1.28	41
1.29-31	30
3.21-26	74

ROMANS (*cont.*)

3.24 ff.	81
4.5	108
5.5	118
5.8	71
5.12-21	37
5.13-14	37
6.3	93
6.23	60
ch. 7	37
7.7-24	81
7.19	13
8.3	58, 73 f.
8.22-23	116

I CORINTHIANS

1.18-25	60
1.30	93
2.9	117
10.16	95
13.12	117
ch. 15	115
15.1-11	60
15.18	122
15.20	122
15.20-23	122
15.35	123
15.36-38	123
15.42-45	38
15.42-46	123
15.50	123

II CORINTHIANS

1.22	115
4.16-5.4	123
5.5	115
5.19	71
5.21	76 f.

GALATIANS
2.20   93, 101
3.13   77, 81
4.4-5   49
5.17   103
6.7   33

EPHESIANS
1.10   113
1.14   115
2.6   93
4.22-24 113

PHILIPPIANS
1.21-24 122
2.7   59
3.9   93, 105

COLOSSIANS
1.27   92

COLOSSIANS (cont.)
2.15   88
3.1   93
3.1-17 103, 113
3.4   92
3.5   29

I THESSALONIANS
4.13-18 122

I TIMOTHY
1.15   8

HEBREWS
2.17   65
3.14   92
9.9-12 51 f.
10.1-4 86
10.5-9 86

HEBREWS (cont.)
10.10-18 86
10.19-20 86
11.8   46

I PETER
1.3-5   116
1.18-19 81, 83
1.23   101

I JOHN
3.2   117
3.8   88

REVELATION
21.1-5   124
21.22   124